The Growing Child

How do children's early physical experiences influence their future health and well-being?

What are the future consequences of a sedentary childhood on life chances and health?

What importance do we place in the UK on sleep, fresh air, good nutrition and movement?

The Growing Child thoughtfully discusses the key principles of children's physical development alongside descriptions of everyday practice. It looks in detail at all aspects of physical development including exercise, diet, sleep and how these link to the development of the whole child.

The book considers key learning dispositions such as perseverance, determination, confidence, responsibility, courage and curiosity, and shows how physical play helps to develop children's organisational skills, team work, risk management, communication and raises their self-esteem. Drawing on the author's own experience of running a Forest School nursery, the book aims to help practitioners to:

- create rich and stimulating play environments that enable children to learn, make connections and explore using their whole bodies;
- reflect on their own teaching methods to encourage children's engagement, motivation and creativity through effective observation and planning;
- engage with parents and carers to help support children's learning at home whilst maintaining the values of the family;
- celebrate the uniqueness of each child and provide learning experiences that are appropriate for individuals with particular learning needs, be they physical, emotional or cognitive, to ensure that every child has an equal opportunity to succeed.

The first seven years of life provide distinct opportunities to lay the foundations for a positive, successful and happy life; it is essential that this is underpinned with a sound knowledge of child development. Emphasising the importance of understanding the theory that underpins children's physical development, this accessible text shows practitioners how they can use this knowledge to provide learning opportunities that nourish children's health, learning and well-being.

Clair Steve is Senior Lecturer in Early Years at Canterbury Christ Church University, U

Foundations of Child Development
Series Editor: Pamela May

An understanding of child development is at the heart of good early years practice. The four books in this exciting new series each take a detailed look at a major strand of child development – cognitive, social, physical and emotional – and aim to provide practitioners with the knowledge and understanding they need to plan ways of working with children that are developmentally appropriate. Clearly linking theory to everyday practice they explain why practitioners teach in certain ways and show how they can provide learning experiences that will help children to become competent and enthusiastic learners. Whilst the series allows for an in-depth study of each of the four major areas of development individually, it also demonstrates that they are, in reality, intertwined and indivisible.

Titles in this series:

The Growing Child

Laying the foundations of active learning and physical health

Clair Stevens

Routledge
Taylor & Francis Group

LONDON AND NEW YORK

First published 2013
by Routledge
2 Park Square, Milton Park, Abingdon, Oxon OX14 4RN

Simultaneously published in the USA and Canada
by Routledge
711 Third Avenue, New York, NY 10017

Routledge is an imprint of the Taylor & Francis Group, an informa business

British Library Cataloguing in Publication Data
A catalogue record for this book is available from the British Library

Library of Congress Cataloging in Publication Data
A catalog record for this book has been requested

ISBN: 978-0-415-52339-4 (hbk)
ISBN: 978-0-415-52340-0 (pbk)
ISBN: 978-0-203-55290-2 (ebk)

Typeset in Bembo and Frutiger
by Fakenham Prepress Solutions, Fakenham, Norfolk NR21 8NN

Printed and bound in Great Britain by
TJ International Ltd, Padstow, Cornwall

I tried to teach my child with books,
He gave me only puzzled looks,
I tried to teach my child with words,
They passed him often unheard.
Despairingly, I turned aside,
'How shall I teach this child?' I cried.
Into my hands he put the key,
'Come', he said 'play with me!'

Anonymous

Contents

Acknowledgements

Sincere thanks go to the children and staff of Manor House Nursery School, Margate, Darland Preschool, Gillingham and Tinkerbells at Iwade who so generously shared their thoughts, experiences and ideas.

Special thanks also go to three important colleagues: Pam May for her belief, encouragement and reassurance, Toni Buchan for sharing the journey and bringing the compass and Rebecca Hogben for constantly reminding me of the importance of the work we do with young children. Additional thanks go to John May for his unending editorial support.

And to my children and husband who remain life's greatest teachers. You continue to show me the way.

Introduction to the series

Let us begin by considering two situations with which we are all probably familiar. Picture, if you will, a sandy beach. The sun is shining, there are gentle waves, little rock pools and a big cave. You have with you children aged six and three, a picnic, towels and buckets and spades. Having chosen your spot you settle down with a rug and a good book, occasionally advising about the construction of the moat for the sand castle or checking out the dragons in the cave. The children come back occasionally to eat or drink and there are the necessary breaks for toilets and ice creams. By 4pm everyone has had a perfect day; you included. No one has cried, there were no squabbles and the children are happily tired enough to ensure a good night's sleep. For days and weeks to come they remember the '*best holiday ever*' as they reminisce about the castles they constructed and the dragons they frightened.

Figure I.1 *Checking out the dragons in the cave*

Now, transfer these same two children to a local supermarket. Imagine the scene here. In my experience the situation starts badly as I issue the firm instruction '*not to touch anything*' as we enter the store, and rapidly goes downhill as one child finds the strawberry yoghurts but the other wants the blueberry ones. I want the mixed pack because they are on offer and a three-way dispute is quickly under way. The smaller child is transferred to the child seat in the trolley, kicking and wailing loudly, and mothers look at me with either sympathy or distaste as this noisy gang proceeds with the shopping. Matters are not helped by the sweets displayed at the checkout at child level, which this cross granny does not consider either of them has deserved.

Why are these two scenarios so very different? The answer lies in the ways that children are hard-wired to learn about their world and to make sense of it. This process is called child development. Children are born with a set of strategies and they apply these strategies wherever they find themselves. One of the ways children learn is by using their senses, so, they need to touch things that interest them to find out about them. That is fine when they are digging in the sand on the beach and collecting shells but not nearly as acceptable when investigating packets of crisps in a supermarket. Children are also hardwired to learn actively, that is, by exploring what is around them. Again, great when looking for dragons in caves but not such a helpful strategy around the aisles in a shop.

These books consider the strategies and other characteristics that all young children have and considers how they can be developed and strengthened in the course of young children's everyday learning.

This series of books is about the process of learning and not the content of learning. Each book describes a separate area of a young child's development and how their relationships and experiences affect the process of that development. Each of the four books takes one aspect and considers it in depth.

> *The Thinking Child: Laying the foundations of understanding and competence.* In this book Pam May considers children's cognitive and intellectual development.
> *The Growing Child: Laying the foundations of active learning and physical health.* In this book I consider children's physical and motor development.
> *The Social Child: Laying the foundations of relationships and language.* In this book Toni Buchan considers children's social and language development.
> *The Feeling Child: Laying the foundations of confidence and resilience.* In this book Maria Robinson considers children's emotional and behavioural development.

Although each book takes one strand of children's development and looks at it separately, this is purely for the purpose of study. In real life, of course, children use all aspects of their development together as they learn to sustain friendships and communicate, grow taller and stronger, deepen their understanding of concepts and morals and grow in self-confidence.

There are thought to be certain characteristics inherent in all children that enable development to proceed effectively. Two of these inborn characteristics, for example, are motivation and autonomy. They need to be matched by an environment which supports their expression and development. Children who thrive and learn well will find their innate characteristics supported by loving and knowledgeable adults in a challenging yet secure environment. This environment will respect the fact that children learn through first-hand experiences, through their senses and that they will usually be doing this actively. This is why the beach provides such an effective learning environment and the supermarket less so. On the beach children can use their strategies of active engagement. They are motivated by the exciting surroundings and can play with considerable freedom and autonomy. Here one can see that their curiosity and capability of finding out about the world are perfectly matched by their environment.

This series will examine these ideas in depth. Established and current research threads through and underpins all the practical suggestions offered here. A theory is no use in isolation; it must always link to what happens to children wherever they are, every day. This is why these books will give the practitioner a chance to consider what implications their reading may have on their practice as well as giving them sound, evidence-based understanding as to why certain ways of teaching and learning can be so successful.

Central to this series are some key beliefs about young children. These include the premise that:

- Children are potentially strong and autonomous learners.
- They need loving and sensitive adults to be their companions.
- Children's view of themselves is key to their success as learners.
- Play is a powerful mechanism that enables children to develop their understandings.
- What children can do should be the starting point of their future learning.

Perhaps these ideas are summed up most clearly in the last of the NAEYC principles:

> Children's experiences shape their motivation and approaches to learning, such as persistence, initiative and flexibility; in turn these dispositions and behaviours affect their learning and development.[1]

These principles are about not *what* children learn but *how* they learn and, consequently, how they are best taught. They are reflected in the new Early Years Foundation Stage.[2]

The review of the EYFS by Dame Clare Tickell places much emphasis on the characteristics of effective learning that we considered above and it is these that we will be examining closely. Each book will discuss those characteristics which apply most closely to the strand of development being considered in the book but, of course, many of these will appear throughout the series. Each book will have chapters reflecting the EYFS emphasis on aspects of effective learning and in particular:

- play and exploration
- active learning
- creativity and critical thinking.

Other chapters will cover aspects of practice common to all settings such as observing children's learning, engaging with families and how to provide for the different learning styles of girls and boys. Finally there will be a chapter that critically examines the notion of school readiness. Each author will explore what it means to be 'school ready' and how we may best support Foundation Stage children to take advantage of all that is on offer for them at key stage one.

Introduction to *The Growing Child*

During the past decade there has been a sharp increase in the concerns relating to children's physical health. In response to this, *The Growing Child* sets out to explore this aspect of physical development in the early years and examines the fundamental links between regular physical play and a child's health and well-being. Recognised as a key or prime area of development by Dame Tickell in the review of the Early Years Framework in 2011, physical health is related to all other aspects of learning. It must not be forgotten that attitudes we adopt in the early years often set the blueprint for later life. Therefore it is vital that in the early years children lay the *'foundations for good health in adult life'*.[1]

This book will invite the reader to reflect on their own childhood and consider the fundamental characteristics associated with being a successful learner as defined in 1994 by Sir Christopher Ball, which are those of:

- motivation
- socialisation
- confidence.[2]

Ball believed the key to successful lifelong learning lay in strengthening children's motivation; in response to this *The Growing Child* will reinforce and at times challenge practitioners to further recognise and foster these 'super skills'. Start Right highlighted the importance of young children establishing a 'can do' attitude and placed emphasis on the acquisition of good social skills; of being involved with others; and having a sense of belonging and emotional well-being. As any good early years practitioner or teacher will recognise, active physical play often incorporates these important dispositions and involves children working closely together.

Physical development is rapid in early childhood and we know from extensive, expanding research that early experiences can affect both the development and biology of multiple organ systems.[3] The book will, therefore, explore the contributions from brain research emphasising the importance of active, physical play. Child development theory has always recognised young children's desires, motivation and physical drive to move their bodies. However, increasingly, practitioners have found it difficult to balance the needs of their children to be outside in challenging environments with the overwhelming responsibility related to health and safety. Another growing concern is the increasing emphasis on academic achievement and the top-down pressure related to this model of education.

The final two chapters will discuss this concept and provide the reader with a vision for education based on first-hand experiences that prepare children for life as well as for school. Sharing the philosophy and ethos of Forest School education, the book will reflect on the experiences of children, parents and practitioners working within nursery, primary schools and Children's Centres.

CHAPTER 1

Setting the scene

> The foundations for virtually every aspect of human development are laid in early childhood. What happens during these early years (starting in the womb) has lifelong effects on many aspects of health and well-being, including mental health, educational achievement and economic status.[1]
>
> *Sir Michael Marmot*

It is difficult for us to comprehend that young children growing up in the twenty-first century in some of the richest, most advanced countries in the Western world are increasingly being denied the essential components necessary to set them up for a healthy and happy life. This statement may sound implausible but research worldwide indicates that children and families are increasingly leading hurried and pressured lifestyles. The results of these influences on a family's lifestyle have undoubtedly led to changes in the upbringing of children. It is important, therefore, that practitioners working in early years settings consider the significance of physical development and health to all-round learning and development. With my background in early years education, but also as a mother, I was recently appalled to see a catalogue selling gym equipment advertised for nursery schools. This equipment was marketed to settings wanting to improve the physical skills and health of their children; the list included exercise bikes, treadmills, rowing machines, a mini-stepper and weight bench. I found myself asking how we could have moved so far from the nature of the English nursery school where play was so highly valued. Few of us surely would think that this is the best way to set young children up for a healthy, rewarding life. Thus *The Growing Child* will explore, with reference to theory and practice, the importance of developing the aspect of physical development in the early years and its close ties in establishing healthy patterns for life.

Although many of us may have few memories from our earliest years, it is these early experiences that often shape and influence many aspects of our adult lives. My own early memories relate to days spent with my brothers on a local beach – freedom seldom given to children today. Brought up on the Kent coast, the beach, surrounding promenades, Victorian gardens and coastland became our playground. They offered rich opportunities throughout the year for physical challenge, sensory stimulation and adventure. Some forty years later my own children use many of the same outdoor spaces to play and explore, but somehow, as a society, it seems that we have lost sight of the importance of these tactile physical experiences.

As early years practitioners, we have a privileged part to play in supporting and enriching the lives of a new generation of young children and their families. These early experiences can set trajectories that affect cognition, relationships, health and well-being for individuals throughout their life. Furthermore, new concerns relating to health and well-being resound today; with physical play and activity seen as an important way of preventing and reducing childhood obesity. The level of obesity in the UK has been portrayed as an epidemic and its impact on children's health and well-being should be a concern for all in society. Many of these concerns focus on poor diets as a major cause but practitioners need to recognise the huge impact that physical activity can play in reversing this trend to obesity. More recently, a return of rickets in parts of England has resulted in a call for children to spend longer periods of time outdoors. The disease had all but died out some eighty years ago but is now returning. It is caused by low levels of vitamin D generated in the body from sunshine and particular types of foods. It is reported that children from all backgrounds are now being affected, a change from the Victorian times when only the poor seemed at risk.

Studying early childhood

The study of how young children grow up is not new; numerous educators and philosophers since the time of Plato have expressed an interest in human development. The past 300 years has seen a number of different approaches to teaching and learning influenced by the work of, among others, Rousseau, Pestalozzi, Froebel, Montessori and the McMillan sisters. In particular the interrelationship between education and health was central to Margaret McMillan's philosophy. She started an outdoor nursery school in Deptford in London, for children at risk of developing TB. The nursery promoted good health with fresh air, home-cooked food and daily physical activities.

At the other end of the social spectrum Chelsea Open Air Nursery School was formed in 1929 for over-indulged children, who were described by a benefactor as *'crippled by not being allowed to take exercise'*.[2] The work of these important pioneers has been significant, influencing policy and practice across the world. Additionally, key figures such as Piaget, Bruner, Isaacs, Vygotsky and Malaguzzi have strengthened this debate and highlighted the importance of both adults and the environment in supporting children's healthy development.

However, early years practitioners, in daily contact with young children and families, will inevitably develop their own theories about early childhood development. These will probably evolve and grow from their own experiences as a child, and from the children they encounter. Over time these theories of development will change and will be influenced by their surroundings and by reading and research. Nowhere is this more evident than when early years students and practitioners come together in discussion. This valuable time spent reflecting and exchanging ideas helps to clarify and legitimise what one believes is important for young children in the setting. Drawing on my own experiences with young children, families, practitioners and students this book seeks to challenge the reader to deconstruct and identify key influences related to their beliefs and philosophies about young children's health, well-being and physical development, and how these are promoted in their settings.

Each of the book's chapters will reinforce the idea that the most effective early learning opportunities are those that offer children space, time and effective support, leading to the development of children as independent, self-directed learners. These are essential elements to support physical skills as children require repeated opportunities both to practise and strengthen their muscles, but also to develop the confidence in their ability to learn what their bodies can do for them. Physical development is vitally important for all children but should be viewed holistically, linked to all other areas of a child's development.

Pregnancy and the early years of life are formative years where the foundations of future health and well-being are established, and more importantly for practitioners across both health and education, it is a time when parents are often more open to learning and making changes, including the underpinning of good early years practice as a key aspect. This vitally important work of engaging and working with parents and families is fully discussed in Chapter 6, where the philosophy and practice of Forest School sessions, which run in partnership with children's centres, will be shared, particularly in relation to engaging fathers.

The importance of play

Within the early childhood context, play has long been recognized as the most valuable vehicle for children's learning and development. Play for young children is motivational and demanding, reflecting both social and cultural contexts. High-quality early years environments must be exciting and challenging, offering opportunities for physical risk that are essential for children's healthy growth and development. Yet factors related to health and safety and the threat of litigation seem to place implicit and explicit demands on staff to prevent or limit experiences involving physical risk.

Sadly, environments that offer no potential hazards will undoubtedly not offer children challenge. If a setting is too safe and restricting to children they are likely to become bored and in the long term grow up lacking self-confidence and belief in their own physical ability.[3] Additionally, physical confidence has frequently been linked with more general feelings of competence. Duberry, interestingly, includes this definition: '*To be broad and adventurous*' as a disposition of a good thinker, emphasising the links between a young child confronting physical fears and risks and transferring this to other learning situations.[4] It is through these interactions during play that children experiment and test their bodies; developing dexterity, control and ultimately mastery.

Figure 1.1 *Confronting physical fears*

Chapter 2, entitled 'Play and exploration', will discuss the central role that rich and stimulating play environments have in enabling children to learn, make connections and explore using their whole bodies. It will consider play both indoors and out and challenge practitioners to apply knowledge from key theorists in relation to children's active engagement and participation. Additionally Chapter 8 will draw further on the Forest School approach and its development in the UK, and present evidence from research that suggests children regularly attending these outdoor sessions develop a wealth of important attitudes and physical skills including improved confidence, self-esteem, determination, physical stamina and core strength. Conversely, children who do not develop their physical skills or test their capabilities in early childhood can feel isolated and remain physically inactive throughout life, drawn to the alternative excitement offered by screen technologies.

The contribution of science

The past decade has seen great advances in neuroscience, genomics, molecular biology and the social sciences, leading to a new deeper understanding of how healthy development occurs. Additionally, more recent contributions from brain research support the early years as a critical period for optimising learning. Shore maintains that it is these early play experiences and interactions that actually affect the way the brain develops. The physical environment and the experiences very young children have shape the brain by either creating new pathways or pruning neurons that have not been used or connected. Shore suggests that '*meeting the developmental needs of young children is as much about building a strong foundation for lifelong physical and mental health as it is about enhancing readiness to succeed in school*'.[5]

Movement and motor skills

Movement is now recognised as central to development and learning. Susan Greenfield suggests that if humans weren't designed to move we wouldn't require a brain.[6] In early childhood movement plays a critical role in learning and connecting the two hemispheres of the brain. Repeated opportunities to practise and refine movements forms patterns in the child's brain and connects networks which link emotional thinking with logical thought. It is essential then that movement and play are emphasised as fundamental to learning in the early years as these experiences nourish the brain and trigger connections between the senses, muscular memory, perception and fluidity. New research and knowledge related specifically to early brain development and the importance of the environment have implications for all those working with young children, particularly the very youngest babies and toddlers. It is important therefore to understand that human development is based on the subtle interaction of both nature (biological factors) and nurture (environmental factors).

The book will include references to motor development, which is defined as the process by which a child acquires movement patterns and skills. Gross motor abilities are connected with other physical functions. For example, in order to write properly a child needs the gross motor skill to maintain upper body support as well as have the physical fine motor skills in the hand and wrist relating to dexterity. Practitioners should consider development as a whole but concentrate on opportunities that lend themselves to developing particular skills. Fine motor skills such as dexterity, associated with such tasks as cutting and pencil control, will follow on naturally from the development of gross motor skills such as body movement related to walking, running, maintaining balance, coordination, jumping and reaching. Those working with young babies will witness extraordinary motor development in the first year of life.

Complex developmental changes related to the organisation of movements are evident almost weekly; from a young infant just able to lift their head to a toddler, approximately fifteen months later, who can navigate numerous objects with great excitement to greet a parent or carer, and very soon afterwards feed themselves demonstrating a maturing pincer grip.

Health and equality

Concerns related to health and inequality have been linked to a number of growing anxieties including poorer outcomes in school, higher levels of stress, lack of engagement, behavioural problems and lower life expectancy. Numerous reviews and reports to the Government suggest that health inequalities often repeat themselves over a generation and that early intervention in the first few years is critical if changes are to be long term. Key points from the most important reports are included at the end of this chapter. Tickell's review of the Early Years Foundation Stage framework in 2008 has identified physical development as one of the three prime areas of development.[7] Furthermore Frank Field's independent review on *Poverty and Life Chances* in 2010 recommended that the Foundation years need to be established in the public mind and given equal status to those of primary and secondary school years, making certain that child development and services during those years are clearly understood.[8] Marmot has also stressed the urgency of closing this gap between the stages of education, suggesting that the Foundation years offer the best opportunity to make considerable improvements in life chances for many children.[9] These sentiments were also echoed by the Oxford University research group who published data from the longitudinal study, the Effective Provision of Preschool Education.[10]

National guidelines

Both the Curriculum Guidance for the Foundation Stage, and the subsequent Birth to Three Matters framework, gave clear guidance on developing physical skills from birth. The current Early Years Foundation Stage framework also promotes the idea that young children need daily access to an outdoor area, signifying that this is an important area for learning and development. However, the framework falls short of making an outdoor environment a statutory requirement, suggesting that settings without one should plan daily experiences for children outdoors. This, sadly, is left for early years practitioners to interpret and many do not have the training or do not understand the importance of these opportunities for their children. It takes a great deal of effort to plan, risk assess and staff daily outings away from the setting, and this often prevents children from experiencing all that is possible outdoors. Nevertheless, many early years settings across the UK have been funded by the local authority to improve and develop outdoor spaces, to provide richer more challenging experiences that can stretch and facilitate physical skills.

Furthermore, the framework includes no requirements regarding the length of time children spend outdoors and include the wording 'suitable weather', indicating to staff and parents that weather conditions in England can sometimes be unsuitable. I would argue that young children actively seek the outdoor environment in all weathers and require extended periods outside in order to practise, rehearse, develop interests and explore possibilities. Limited resources can restrict children's play, but by providing a rich variety of larger 'loose parts', such as crates, tyres, ladders, tarpaulins, planks and logs, play can be enriched and support exciting and creative experiences that encourage physical engagement. Gone are the days when planned activities, often considered as 'work' or 'learning', were set up indoors, and play or 'letting off steam' was promoted outdoors. More recently it has been suggested that the outdoor environment should mirror the activities indoors, but while both are equally important and should complement and support the other; they are quite different and offer diverse possibilities.

The importance of child development

A sound knowledge of child development is essential for those working in the early years, in order to support families to establish healthy patterns for life. Physical development starts in the womb and forms the platform on which all subsequent development builds. Future outcomes related to educational success, health, well-being and social skills are strongly dependent on what happens during pregnancy and the first years of life. In May 2011, Edwin Poots, Minister for Health in Northern Ireland, spoke at an early years interventions conference in Belfast. He said that '*A child's early years form the pattern of their future adult life. However, children are not just adults in waiting, destined to become society's future. We have a duty to give children a "now"*'. It appears that governments across the UK recognise that all young children deserve the best start in life and are seeking to support families from pregnancy onwards. However, the focus on 'school readiness' in England needs to be more fully explored and clear guidelines drawn up so parents and practitioners are not sitting children down for long periods with inappropriate, structured school-based activities. This discussion forms the basis of the final chapter of the book with evidence drawn from home and abroad. It argues against the formalisation of these influential years and focuses the argument on the development of dispositions of learning or character skills that are seen by many as fundamental to life-long learning. These include openness, curiosity, resilience, consciousness, extroversion, agreeableness and persistence.

These skills proposed by Claxton and Carr are linked to long-term outcomes such as raising educational achievement, reducing obesity and improving life changes.[11] Evidence gathered from the Perry Preschool Project concluded that conscientiousness, a form of self-control, was the principal indicator of school achievement in the long term. Furthermore, Sir Christopher Ball, author of the Start Right Report, outlined the most important learning in preschool in terms of aspiration, motivation, socialisation and self-esteem. He further defined three essential 'superskills' of learning:

> The art of learning (learning how to learn) is also concerned with the types, or 'super skills' and attitudes, of learning; of which motivation, socialisation and confidence are the most important. These are the fruits of successful early learning.[12]

This chapter started with key words from the Marmot review, *Fair Society, Healthy Lives*. It is the job of each and every one of us working with young children and families to make it our highest priority to 'give every child the best start in life'. I hope *The Growing Child* enables you to see the potential in every child, to be brave in your approach and to light the fire of achievement in yourself and all the children you encounter.

CHAPTER 2

Play and exploration

Early years settings play a key role in providing enabling environments which can help contribute towards young children achieving their daily physical activity requirements for health and well-being.[1]

The next three chapters of *The Growing Child* will discuss and consider how young children learn, rather than the emphasis being placed on the content or curriculum of learning and development. These central commitments to 'Play and Exploration', 'Active Learning' and 'Creativity and Critical Thinking' are identified in the Early Years Foundation Stage (EYFS) framework[2] and have been highlighted as quality indicators for effective learning. The Tickell review of the EYFS released in March 2011 fully support these indicators as the three 'characteristics of effective teaching and learning' and these have been endorsed in the new framework, EYFS 2012.[3] This focus is significant as it divides the 'content or curriculum' from the 'process of learning', and allows practitioners to incorporate their understanding and knowledge of child development into their practice in order to support each child's progress. By recognising and acknowledging how young children learn and how skills are rehearsed and mastered, practitioners are empowering children to become confident, capable life-long learners. As a mother of six and an educator of young children for almost thirty years working with a range of families and settings, I have had countless opportunities of observing young children at play. These direct and extensive first-hand experiences have helped me to recognise, value and now question the opportunities that are on offer to young children relating to physical development, sensory stimulation and their interaction with the environment.

It is widely accepted by governments across the UK that all young children deserve the best start in life and each body recognises, within their current legislation, the central place of play in the early years. Go into any setting, large or small, and practitioners will endorse and engage in discussions asserting the benefits of learning through play. Evidence suggests, however, that it is down to the knowledge and skills of those individuals leading and planning young children's daily experiences to place the child at the centre of their work, with all the challenges and difficulties this may bring. In this book, as in others from the series, physical development will not be viewed in isolation but holistically. As children do not separate learning into boxes, therefore neither should we. In addition this chapter will reflect on the changes in society and the limitations they impose on natural play and exploration. Play is so significant to optimal child development that it has been accepted and endorsed by the United Nations as a Right of Every Child.[4] However, regardless of the well-established benefits associated with play in childhood, the opportunities for free unstructured play have been markedly reduced for many children. Therefore it is important to carefully consider young children's physical needs in relation to exciting, engaging 'real play' as they grow up in the ever advancing era of screen technology and 'virtual play'.

With the health and physical development of young children so high on the political agenda it is ironic that, at the start of the last century, similar concerns relating to the health and life chances of young working-class children were also under the political spotlight. At this time several pioneers emerged recognising the vital links between a healthy body and a healthy mind.[5] Key influences of these early nursery pioneers will be explored in this chapter, particularly in relation to health, physical environments and play. It is important for us all working with young children and families to be able to articulate our guiding principles, not simply relying on our personal experiences and beliefs. Therefore the principles of early learning identified by Tina Bruce[6] have been included in order to support staff groups to discuss and establish principles in relation to practice. These principles were formulated using evidence drawn together from the most eminent psychologists and early years pioneers and they root our work firmly in child development theory. Reflecting on the work of these pioneers, who worked determinedly over many years to improve the lives of the children, and often the families they worked with, you gain an understanding of the transformative nature of early years practice. A number of themes and discussions may emerge across the series; nevertheless, this book will offer practitioners working with young children across a variety of settings the opportunities to question practice, consider alternatives and reflect on Claxton and Carr's term '*ready, willing and able to learn*'[7] rather than the more recently discussed term 'school readiness'.

Playing to learn – learning to play, establishing a pattern for life

> Physically active play improves muscle control and co-ordination, strength and endurance, and may promote fat reduction and body temperature regulation. Rough-and-tumble play usually involves playing with others and is related to social skills, status and emotional control.[8]

Play and playfulness may vary in its interpretation and customs culturally, but around the world children and adults learn and engage in their world as players. Consider your understanding and experiences of play, both as a child and an adult. When we hear the phrase 'it's child's play', is this suggesting perhaps that a child's play is easy? Microsoft used this term in a very successful commercial to demonstrate the ease with which customers could learn to use PowerPoint. Perhaps this suggests that 'child's play' is indeed exploratory and fulfilling, leading to the emergence of new skills and knowledge. However, those of us who see young children engaged in play every day understand that it is difficult to define, but would endorse play's naturalness, fluidity and enjoyment. The last decade has seen an explosion in new play-based activities, promoted, set up and aimed at adults linked to recreation, self-esteem and team building. Think about the new shops that have emerged in every shopping centre offering vast ranges of play props and gadgets.

So what is driving this new playful approach? Role play as a teaching tool is now actively encouraged in both further and higher education as a way of engaging students, as experiential learning is known to be much more powerful than instruction. Alongside this, new outdoor adventure 'play' activities such as 'Paint Ball' and 'Go Ape' have been established to encourage groups of adults and teens to get dirty, take risks, be adventurous, challenge themselves and support others. Consider some of the most successful companies in the twenty-first century: Google, Apple, IDEO, and you will begin to formulate a picture of adults paid and encouraged to engage in serious, collaborative play. These companies have recognised the serious benefits of play in terms of creativity, innovation and engagement and have actively encouraged staff to play together in spaces designed and set up for play and exploration. Developing such skills in the fast-moving economy of the twenty-first century is seen by many as a priority.

Those of us working and supporting staff in the early years regularly articulate and acknowledge the benefits of play in terms of young children's development, but how often do we really stop and observe play in all its complexity? So, as adults, it seems that we are seeking physical 'play' not only in terms of sports and recreation but also for the collaborative nature of playing together to develop ideas, build better relationships and to support health and fitness. Why then should these opportunities be undervalued in terms of developing our youngest children? Surely play belongs to them, it is theirs and we must strive to extend the opportunities and environments that support it as the foundation of all learning and development.

Water, water everywhere

After a particularly wet night the children entered the preschool garden eager to explore the exciting environment created by the rain. That morning there was light rain and the children wore waterproof clothing and boots. Their attention was drawn to water collected in puddles on top of the sand pit and in the pile of guttering left by the children the previous afternoon. The garden offered many new opportunities for exploration that morning, snail trails and silvery patterns from slugs were evident and spider webs glistening with water filled every corner. The children, all aged three and four, demonstrated their growing knowledge associated with water and rain:

'I hear the rain sometimes, it's on my roof, near the kitchen, it makes my dog bark'
'Spiders hide from the rain, it's slippery, look'
'I can hear it, listen it's tapping', *'I think it's drinking it'*
'Dogs drink it', *'Snails drink it too'*.

As one child moves a tyre and uncovers a round patch of dry ground he announces: *'The rain missed this bit, it was hiding'*.

The tyre then becomes a new fascination to the children; as they roll it the water trapped inside is moved creating new interesting sounds, questions and dimensions to their explorations. *'How can we get it out?'*, *'Where is it?'*

While these children expressed their thinking using verbal questions, others demonstrated their thinking through their actions; one took a spoon and a bucket and began collecting water from wherever it had collected. Noticing his intent a practitioner went inside and returned with a large sponge. She demonstrated to him how water could be soaked up in the sponge then squeezed out into his bucket. He seemed to love this idea, abandoning the spoon and was observed soaking up as much water as possible to fill his bucket. Later, once content with his quantity, he returned to find his abandoned spoon and eagerly stirred what had now become his concoction. Leaves, pebbles and grass had been added to his mixture and he offered it to anyone who wanted a taste.

The opportunities provided for stimulating play and exploration, simply by exploring the outdoor environment every day regardless of the weather, are immense and often missed. The document *Learning, Playing and Interacting*[9] reinforces the idea that *'practitioners cannot plan children's play, because this would work against the choice and control that are central features of play. Practitioners can and should plan for children's play, however, by creating high-quality learning environments, and ensuring uninterrupted periods for children to develop their play.'*

Another wonderful example of early years practitioners using a shower of rain was described by Dorothy Selleck following a visit to the Reggio Emilia centres in Northern Italy.[10] She describes her lasting memories of toddlers playing in the nursery garden, running around with ribbons of packaging tucked into the back of their dungarees. Her descriptions of them, *'strutting like peacocks with folded tail feathers, cooing and hooting with excitement as they trailed their tails through puddles'*, is delightful and captures the awe and wonder of young children as they engage excitedly trying to understand the intriguing patterns created by their movements.

Reflect then on your own childhood: what features of play and exploration flood your most intense memories? As a child growing up in the sixties very close to the coast, mine are predominantly outdoors and include an abundance of smells; of the damp, dark lookouts in the chalk face, rock pools full of treasures that changed as they filled with water as the tide rose. Victorian coastal gardens that included formal and wild areas, slopes, steps, sand, shingle, grass and flowering shrubs that would release scent for much of the year. These playgrounds, without toys or areas designed and equipped with young children in mind, offered an abundance of play opportunities to the groups of local children who frequented these spaces, creating and recreating scenarios of play. The multitude of what Simon Nicholson calls 'loose parts'[11], that is, stones, shells, sticks, seaweed, glass, wood and rope to name just a few, were evident in these spaces. They became the supporting props that enriched and extended narrative, added dimension and enabled creative and divergent thinking. However, we must ask ourselves, are these memories primarily imprinted due to the natural environment and the multi-sensory elements associated with them? Or was it that the play here was moving, challenging, child-led and creative, offering real problems, encouraging children to solve problems, think about risk management and indulge in physical dexterity? Tim Gill, author and one of the UK's leading thinkers on childhood, recently questioned whether the outdoor child is doomed to extinction.[12] He suggests that most adults, or certainly those over twenty-five, spent much of their childhood playing outdoors in natural places.

Most early years settings and schools have prioritised the creation of safe, accessible outdoor areas, but sadly many of the more natural, challenging aspects have been removed and replaced by the 'KFC' version: the kit, fence and carpet. This undoubtedly restricts the physical benefits of play as children soon become bored, uninspired and de-motivated. If we recognise and accept that play is crucial for children's health and well-being then we must all strive to give them back the experiences we once took for granted. Unstructured physical play in changing natural surroundings is essential for today's children, particularly those who find themselves spending long periods of time in a childcare setting. It not only contributes to cognitive, physical, social and emotional well-being but provides daily opportunities for children to take responsibility, work collaboratively and start to access risks for themselves.

Dr Len Almond, one of the co-authors of the *UK Physical Activity Guidelines for Early Years*, suggests that young children who can walk unaided should be physically active for three hours a day, a surprising length of time for many of us I'm sure, but this amount of time is in line with many other international countries. He further states that the vast range of physical skills that are learnt in early childhood will be matched at no other time of life.

He recommends that children (those who can walk) should every day:

- use large muscle groups, such as the back, shoulders, legs and arms
- engage in more energetic forms of physical activity, such as running and chasing games
- practise a wide range of different movements, such as locomotor (jumping, hopping, skipping, dancing), stability (balancing, riding a bike or scooter, climbing) and object control skills (kicking, catching, throwing, rolling)
- experience a variety of play spaces and equipment
- set up their own play areas such as an off-the-ground balancing track
- make up their own physically active play such as jumping games
- have fun and feel good about themselves and what they can do.[13]

Reflecting on the work of key pioneers

> All true education is primarily physiological. It is concerned not with books, but
> with nervous tissue.[14]

The understanding and knowledge of play and its complex relationship to learning
and development have been influenced over many years by the work of numerous
educationalists, psychologists, researchers and practitioners. Each has their own
interpretation, but universally it is accepted that play is the most successful vehicle
for learning in the Foundation years. What has been established from the history
of early childhood research is an accepted set of principles defined by Tina
Bruce that draws together the thinking of key figures such as Pestalozzi, Froebel,
Montessori, Steiner, McMillan, Piaget, Vygotsky and Bruner. These guiding
principles help practitioners working today to express and reflect on the values,
philosophies and practice underpinning their work. There are interesting parallels
between these core principles defined by Tina Bruce and the more recent work
of Daniel Goleman looking at 'emotional intelligence'. Goleman's work identified
key aspects of self-control, enthusiasm, persistence and self-motivation, suggesting
that these could and should be taught to children.[15]

In 1987, Tina Bruce adapted the following principles of play from various
research sources:

1   The best way to prepare children for their adult life is to give them what they
    need as children, therefore childhood is seen as valid in itself, not simply a
    preparation for adulthood.
2   Children are whole people who have feelings, ideas and relationships with
    others, and who need to be physically, mentally, morally and spiritually healthy.
3   Learning should not be separated; young children learn in an integrated way
    and not in neat, tidy compartments. Everything links.
4   Children learn best when they are given appropriate responsibility, allowed
    to make errors, decisions and choices, and respected as autonomous learners.
    Intrinsic motivation is valued.
5   Self-discipline is emphasised. Indeed, this is the only kind of discipline worth
    having. Reward systems are very short term and do not work in the long term.
    Children need their efforts to be valued.
6   There are especially receptive periods of learning at different stages of devel-
    opment, when children are especially able to learn particular things such as
    language.
7   What children can do (rather that what they cannot do) is the starting point of
    a child's education.
8   There is an inner life in the child that develops and emerges when conditions
    are favourable (imagination, creativity, language).
9   Relationships with other people (both adults and children) are of central
    importance in a child's life.

10 Education is about three things: the child, the context in which learning takes place, and knowledge itself.[16]

These principles should guide our everyday planning as they are just as relevant today as when they were first devised.

A quick historical tour

Friedrich Froebel became one of the most important educationalists of the nineteenth century. As a young child, he spent a great deal of time playing alone in the gardens around his home; experiences that led to an understanding, love and respect for nature and gardens. At fifteen, Froebel studied forestry, geometry, land surveying and valuation, taking up his first post as a forester in 1802. After attending Frankfurt University where he studied architecture, he began teaching under Johann J. Pestalozzi, who was himself a much respected educator of the day. Unlike other schools at the time, Pestalozzi would welcome the children of the poor into his school, including orphans, believing that children must be active participants in their own learning. It was not until 1837, when Froebel was fifty-five, that he founded his own school calling it a 'kindergarten' or 'children's garden'. This expression and vision for young children incorporated play and exploration in environments that offered time, space and beauty. Froebel considered his approach to education as 'self-activity', allowing the child to be led by their own interests and giving time for them to freely explore. The practitioner's role, therefore, was to be a guide rather than to lead learning.

Margaret and her sister Rachel McMillan are highlighted here for the important work and writing that they undertook over their lifetime and for the contribution they made to the debates related to early childhood development. Margaret was a socialist journalist who witnessed the effects of extreme poverty firstly in Bradford and later in Deptford. The poor housing, food and sanitation were described vividly to her readers in repeated articles. She was concerned primarily with their health and identified three themes: growth, food and dirt. This formed the basis of McMillan's theory of a working-class childhood. In 1892 Margaret joined Dr James Kerr, the school medical officer for Bradford, to begin the first medical review of elementary school children in Britain. Together they published a report identifying these problems and started a campaign to improve the health of children; campaigning for bathrooms, improved ventilation and free school meals. Margaret, a keen political journalist, was perfectly placed to raise important questions regarding infant mortality; sharing research linking birth weight to working hours and publicising the value of breastfeeding. Those working with young children and families today, particularly with a focus on early intervention and health, will recognise many of the same campaigns as they continue to be current concerns and form the basis of interventions.

While the McMillans sisters' interest and initial work began in Bradford, the first open-air camp school opened in 1911 in Depford. Initially this was a girls' camp for children aged from six years; a second boys' camp followed in 1912 set up in St Nicholas' church yard. These open-air camp schools provided regular home-cooked meals, fresh air and access to daily washing facilities. Baths and showers were encouraged and seen as a necessity alongside education and nurture. The baby camp was not opened until 1914 offering twenty-nine places for children under five years of age; this essentially was the beginning of the Open-Air Nursery School. The McMillan sisters read widely and were influenced by the work of an important French doctor Edouard Seguin. His influences on their work can be seen in the importance of the physical space of a school, to the food and clothing children were given and particularly on the role of women as nurturers and caregivers. Indeed, Steedman suggests that it was from Seguin that the McMillans learnt an '*educational vocabulary of love, nurture and physical activity*'.[17] While Margaret and Rachael McMillan were campaigning politically and looking at the physical needs of young children in England in a new way, Maria Montessori, one of the first female doctors in Italy, was using her medical knowledge to enhance the life chances of those children described at the time as 'abnormal' or 'retarded'. Montessori had trained under Edouard Seguin and began her work using his physiological method, that of exercising the muscles to encourage behavioural change. He believed that by actively encouraging children to use their hands to manipulate objects, intelligence would be stimulated. As a doctor passionately concerned with social reform, Montessori combined the ideas of Seguin and Jean Marc Itard – those of 'education of the senses' and 'education of movement' – to form her own educational model. Her own ideas were shaped by the children she observed in the institutions in Rome as they crawled around on the floor after a meal playing. She sensed that the activity of exploring with their hands to find crumbs of bread was not simply driven by hunger but a way of trying to understand their environment. This led her to design a range of items to be made available to the children specifically for stimulating the senses as the inspiring French doctors Seguin and Itard had done before her.

Following her success of working with children considered uneducable, Montessori turned her attention to young children living in the poorest areas in Rome, opening her first Casa de Bambini, Children's House, in San Lorenzo in 1906. Her real world, full of sensorial resources and activities, is today still part of any good Montessori prepared environment. Montessori's understanding of child development and her foresight are captured in *The Absorbent Mind* published in 1946. Here she reaches the conclusion that: '*The greatest development is achieved during the first years of life, and therefore it is then that the greatest care should be taken. If this is done then the child does not become a burden; he will reveal himself as the greatest marvel of nature.*'[18] It is important to consider here Montessori's vision of the prepared environment for young children.

In our settings, how often do we look at the environment in terms of the children or babies using it? When did we last consider how the set-up and flow of the room aids or restricts physical development? For example, are there opportunities for toddlers to experience different surfaces and gradients and easily reach a chosen destination? Think about reducing the more recognisable 'toys' and replacing them with more natural collections of resources such as treasure baskets and interest boxes, designed and put together to stimulate the senses and encourage manipulation.

Another key influence on the principles which underpin our work in the early years is that of Susan Isaacs, a psychologist and teacher who herself was highly influenced by Froebel's ideas and principles. She avidly promoted the benefits of outdoor play, valuing exploratory first-hand experiences as particularly beneficial to young children. The Malting House School, where Isaacs' work was established, first opened as an experimental nursery school in 1924. It provided a well-resourced garden and an approach to learning that actively engaged young children with real experiences. Isaacs maintained that the school's philosophy would produce children with a '*scientific attitude to life*' and argued that each child should be supported to develop intellectual curiosity and strength of character. The school promoted scientific observation of plants and animals, utilising the garden to grow and harvest their own vegetables and fruit. In addition she felt that they should be '*as physically healthy as possible*' suggesting that the best way of preparing a person for life would be to '*safeguard his zest for life*'. In fact the children at the Malting House School regularly used real tools, made fires and climbed trees, activities now identified in the development of the Forest School approach.[19] Isaacs' philosophy and pedagogical approach brought together a rich inviting environment with openness, on the part of the staff, to respond and be led by the children's interests. Mary-Jane Drummond claims that the children at the Malting House School would be 'more active, more curious, more creative, more exploratory, and more inventive than they could have been in any ordinary school'.[20]

Figure 2.1 *More active, more curious*

Exciting real play versus the world of virtual play

Anyone who has seen young children appear hypnotised by screen technology will know that this can be an extraordinarily compelling medium. The technology offers exciting, stimulating, fast-moving images that young children are drawn to. It is understandable that children will be attracted to the constantly changing range of digital media on offer. Research from Europe in 2010 suggests 'the average seven-year-old will have already watched screen media for more than one full year of 24-hour days'.[21] However, we must take great care in the early years to minimize the amount of time that under-fives spend being sedentary, remembering they are forming habits for life, establishing brain structures and building self-confidence in their own abilities. When I ask my teenage sons why they and their friends play for so long in virtual worlds their responses are often '*to have fun*'. Tim Gill, author of *No Fear: Growing Up in a Risk Adverse Society*, suggests that '*although there is a widely-held view that children grow up faster today, in fact their lives are far more controlled than they were 30 years ago*'.[22] This desire to control and keep children safe has increasingly led children to find fun online or in front of a screen, safe and where adults know where they are.

The discussions around the positive benefits of using screen media for young children can indeed be persuasive; however they take little consideration of young children's physical development and health. The British Office of Communication reported in 2011 that '*children are watching more TV than ever . . . viewing figures increasing by two hours per week since 2007*'.[23] This increase was also seen in the use of computer games and games consoles, again an increase in use of almost two hours. The debate and conflict between the advocates of screen technology in the Foundation years, and the growing warnings from paediatrics and biologists, centre on the age at which young children are exposed to and the time they spend relating to the screen. Some believe that to refrain from introducing young children to these experiences puts them at a developmental or educational disadvantage. The debate and discussion around the use of screen technology will continue, with staff teams and parents needing to accept that it is easy sometimes to give in to children, particularly as the pull of the screen can be so engaging. However, children's enthusiasm and enjoyment of active physical play, particularly outdoors, is our responsibility and we must make it equally appealing. Evidence collected from children in early years settings reviewing their experiences of the EYFS reported that most children talked about their sense of physical competency, sharing enthusiastically their enjoyment of physically active play. However, it was found that the children who were least enthusiastic, who were stating a preference for less active play, had a physical environment that was limited: '*I only like watching television. I like sleeping and building, and sitting colouring and drawing.*' Interestingly, the setting here was noted as offering the most limited outdoor play opportunities, with only four children able to play outside at a given time.[24] In conclusion, then, it is our responsibility as early years practitioners to ensure that the opportunities offered to young children are exciting, challenging and physical, offering the same stimulation and appeal as the virtual worlds.

Challenges and dilemmas

- It is clear then that daily opportunities for extended periods of active play and exploration can increase the locomotor physical activity in young children. This includes any activities that promote bodily movement resulting in energy expenditure. In order for these to be most beneficial it is important for staff to consider the frequency, intensity, duration and type of activity in order to develop both large and small muscle groups.

- Consider the amount of time young children spend outdoors throughout the year. Active play and exploration outside should be encouraged and planned each day regardless of the weather; remember there is no such thing as unsuitable weather, only unsuitable clothing.

- How are the environments prepared for babies and young children? Think carefully about the sensory aspects of your resources and the layout of each space in terms of physical development.

- Equipment can become damaged or fall out of favour. It is worth taking at least an annual audit of your resources and dispose of what is not needed (be ruthless!).

- Screen technology can be appealing to young children, so a debate about how the use of IT and technology can support play and exploration will produce a policy. Use IT to complement active play rather than as a substitute to keep children entertained.

CHAPTER 3

Active learning

The young of all creatures cannot keep their bodies still or their tongues quiet: they always want to move and cry out; some are leaping and skipping and overflowing with playfulness and pleasure, and others uttering all sorts of cries.[1]

Plato

Observe any young animal or child and you will be both exhausted by their continual movement and drawn by their magnetic playfulness. Babies and young children are naturally active, interested learners, eager to interact and make sense of the world they are born into. Reflect on the competence and determination of very young children when exploring in an environment not naturally set up for play: the kitchen. This new playroom offers an abundance of new opportunities and challenges, with the possibilities for hands-on exploration both exciting and motivating. The fridge, cupboards, bin and anything else within reach are explored as a scientist, engineer or chef would test any new design. Items are opened and closed, tasted, banged, posted, taken apart and reconfigured. As parents we may not fully appreciate the science, investigation and assessment involved in tipping, banging, mixing, opening and tasting the contents of the fridge or bin, and at times wonder at our children's dexterity and problem solving as they work out new ways of reaching items placed higher on the shelves. But this motivation and perseverance are vital tools for learning and are evident even in the youngest children.

Infants and toddlers are active learners from birth and are intrinsically motivated to explore the world around them, inspecting and engaging with the people and objects in their path and gathering information in the process. Even the youngest child makes active choices and decisions, developing both cognitively and physically as he or she interacts with objects and people. This *'playing, doing, thinking and learning'*,[2] as defined by Christine Stephen, is led by children's active engagement in rich environments that are *'affording, inviting or potentiating' supporting the conditions for robust learning'*.[3] It is this desire to learn, to be interested and actively involved that is now recognised as one of the most important drivers for life-long learning.

Increasingly, pedagogy underpinning practice in the early years has recognised the importance of an active play-based approach frequently described as active learning. Drawing on the previous Curriculum Guidance and the Birth to

Three Matters framework, the British Government implemented the Early Years Foundation Stage framework and accompanying guidance in 2007, placing an explicit emphasis on children as active learners from birth to five. This emphasis has now been further strengthened with active learning identified as one of the three characteristics of effective learning and teaching. However, it is important for those of us working daily with young children that we do not confuse 'teaching' with simply conveying our own knowledge, learning and understanding. It is much more intense and usable if the children have first-hand experiences of doing, and finding out for themselves. This chapter offers practitioners practical examples of active learning underpinned by theory in relation to physical development and motivation. It will draw on the work of several key theorists, taking account of their differing ideas and philosophies in relation to child development and the role of the adult.

Previously it was believed that babies developed physically following a fixed timetable, governed by changes in the brain. However, more recent research has suggested that developmental milestones are reached through a complex inter-action involving the brain, the baby's growing awareness of its own body and the environment. This new research is contributing to *'the emerging view of infants as active participants in their own motor-skill acquisition, in which developmental change is empowered through infants' everyday problem-solving activities'*.[4] Below are some of the current universally accepted theories upon which active learning is based:

> In active learning settings, children engage with an abundance and variety of materials that challenge their thinking skills and support their sensory, whole-body approach to learning.[5]

> Children learn best through physical and mental challenges. Active learning involves other people, objects, ideas and events that engage and involve children for sustained periods.[6]

The Scottish Curriculum for Excellence further defines active learning as:

> Learning which engages and challenges children's thinking using real-life and imaginary situations. It takes full advantage of the opportunities for learning presented by:

> - spontaneous play
> - planned purposeful play
> - investigating and exploring
> - events and life experiences
> - focused learning and teaching.[7]

The Welsh Foundation Phase additionally supports the importance of play and active learning suggesting that it cannot be *'emphasised strongly enough'*. They also state that, *'The curriculum and environment should be planned and structured to enable children to be active learners. Children should have opportunities to explore their learning environment and to learn new skills as well as repeating, practising and refining skills they have already acquired. It is important that children have plenty of occasions to experiment with resources, to try to solve problems as well as selecting their own materials for an activity.*[8]

The HighScope approach

The HighScope Perry Preschool Study was developed and implemented in America in the 1960s by David Weikart and his colleagues, but was highly influenced by the cognitive developmental work of Jean Piaget as well as the progressive educational philosophy of John Dewey who was described by many as the father of education. The foundation of the HighScope approach to early childhood education was the acceptance that active learning was central to development and that active learning occurs most successfully in settings that provide developmentally appropriate learning opportunities. Additionally, the HighScope method views learning as a social experience involving significant interactions among children and adults. These social exchanges occur in the context of real-life activities that children plan and initiate themselves, or within adult-initiated experiences that offer children individual expression, choice and leadership. Consider the following example:

Following several days of high winds the children entered the garden area to discover a complete bird's nest that had been dislodged from a nearby tree or high ledge. The nest became the centre of attention with children wanting to touch, hold, feel and dismantle the entangled twigs, grass, moss and feathers. Using a tray to capture the structure the children dismantled the nest, discussing, reflecting and evaluating the size, shape, strength, position and use of the nest. The adult added extended vocabulary and provided a commentary for their exploration, leaving the children to lead the investigation. They reflected on the way the nest was built and described the patterns created by the woven twigs. The practitioner left the nest for the children to explore all week, gathering their thoughts, questions and ideas for further planning. To support the children's obvious interest the practitioner printed off several photographs of different nests which varied in size, structure, composition and location. Some incorporated mud; others were very neat and spherical, built with symmetry and precision while others were an untidy mass of twigs. The children used the photographs during the next few days to explore the local woodland for suitable materials, bringing back bags of new construction materials. As these were emptied into the garden the children began categorising the items by length, shape, strength and size. Supported by the adults, small groups of children worked together to build their own nests of varying complexities and size. Each was unique to the group and as they worked the children discussed, evaluated, reflected and at times disagreed. The 'nest project' extended over several weeks with the children returning to their own creations, adding, changing and playing with the structures. One nest was big enough for children to climb into and became a fixture of the garden for several months.

Consider where this interest and enthusiasm could extend in terms of planning? This project demonstrated the importance of active learning but equally confirms the significance of supporting adults, who see opportunities for learning everywhere and have faith in children's curiosity and exploration, allowing children to set their own agenda and timescale.

An important element of the active learning process as defined by Weikart was the need for children first to interact 'thoughtfully' with their world then reflect on their actions. A key component of the HighScope approach is the 'plan, do, review' aspect of practice. Children's knowledge and understanding of the world develops as they test ideas and seek answers to their questions. Think about a young baby reaching for an item in a treasure basket. At this exploratory stage they are simply asking, '*What is this, what do I know about it, what can I do with it?*' As they clutch an item to be manipulated, sucked, chewed and tasted, it may be dropped or discarded close by. The resulting reflection on the action enables the child to begin to construct a personal understanding of objects. Some items may roll away while others will remain stationary; some round objects are cold and reflect the light while others are highly scented and visually bright; others create sounds when banged together. The child's actions together with the reflections on those actions lead to the development of understanding and thought. Therefore it is both the physical activity of play and exploration and the mental activity of interpretation that lead to new connections and learning.

The five ingredients of active learning adapted from HighScope 2011

Below are some of the guidelines issued by the HighScope researchers aimed at supporting practitioners to ensure that learning is rich and active:

1 *Materials*: these should be abundant, age-appropriate and sensory. Provide plenty of open-ended resources that the child can use in a variety of ways. Loose parts and scrap materials provide children with multiple opportunities to explore. Learning develops directly out of the child's direct action with the materials and the reflection that follows.
2 *Manipulation*: the child requires repeated opportunities to explore (with all of their senses), manipulating, combining and transforming their environments inside and out.
3 *Choice*: it should be the child who chooses what they want to do. Intrinsic motivation keeps children interested and enthusiastic. Since learning results from the child's attempts to pursue personal interests and goals, the opportunity to choose activities and materials is essential.
4 *Child communication, language, and thought*: the child communicates his or her needs, feelings, discoveries and ideas through motions, gestures, facial expressions, sounds, sign language, and words. Practitioners should value, attend to and encourage all forms of communication and language.

5   *Adult scaffolding*: adults establish and maintain trusting relationships with each child in their care. Adults recognise and encourage each child's intentions, actions, interactions, communications, explorations, problem solving and creativity.

Putting the theory into practice

> In furthering our understandings of children and their development, it is wise to remember that children function as whole and complete human beings…although it is often convenient to subdivide children's development into various sections either by domain or by age stage, the holistic nature of child development means there is an equal need to stress the continuity of development, since it is the accumulation of experiences from every aspect of development that creates what the child is today.[9]

Think back to times in your life when you were physically learning a completely new skill or trying to persuade your body to move in the way you wanted it to. Now in our late forties, my husband and I have started to learn to dance. What is quite clear is that interest, motivation and enthusiasm are important, but require regular input with an expert offering structure, guidance and support. This then allows us to embed the movements in relation to our partner as well as establishing how each dance fits together in time with the music. Importantly, in order to improve and become 'dancers', in some sense of the word, we then need repeated opportunities to practise, rehearse, adapt and develop. Over time, movements become established within the muscular memory and thoughts can turn to developing other concepts such as musicality and expression. Piaget would suggest that this is part of human functioning, heavily reliant on a principle he called adaptation. This is the process of learning from the environment, modifying and changing to adjust within it. Fine-tuning, he believed, comes about through the complementary processes of assimilation and accommodation.

When new experiences challenge their previous knowledge, the child has to create a new set of understandings to accommodate what they have just experienced. Assimilation occurs when we utilise and combine something from the world around us, incorporating it into our pre-existing mental structures. A child therefore coming across a new stimulus tries to associate it with their previous experience. For example, a baby who is comfortable, holding and sucking the breast or bottle, will happily explore and assimilate any other stimulus into its cognitive framework. Any item at this stage of development will automatically be explored with the mouth using pre-existing knowledge and responses. However, when the baby experiences something different, this must be assimilated in order to be recognised in the future. Piaget maintained that this was how learning took place. By accommodation or adjusting to new experiences the child is constantly updating the previous mental framework to fit new information.

Figure 3.1 *Learning from the environment*

Watch young children playing with sand: having been given the opportunity and materials to explore in the sand pit, they have established that sand passes easily through a sieve or flows freely down the sand wheel into the container below. However, add water to the sand and the results are quite different. The properties of the sand have been changed and the established rules must now be modified. Piaget believed children continually seek a state of equilibrium or balance. But as they encounter increasingly complex situations this balance is upset, resulting in new learning, or threads of thinking being created. Put simply, you cannot experience something for the child, as they must construct knowledge for themselves. By giving children direct first-hand opportunities to investigate, discover and create fresh concepts we are allowing new connections to be formed and motivation for learning to be increased.

These first-hand experiences help to:

- motivate and sustain learning
- stimulate discussion and enquiry
- support developing independence and thinking
- develop physical skills and bodily awareness
- establish boundaries and rules
- support language and communication skills
- build concentration
- develop positive attitudes and self-esteem
- consolidate learning.

While many believe Piaget saw young children as *lone scientists*, learning and discovering the world for themselves, Vygotsky's image was centred more on the notion of children as apprentices, helped by the accumulated experiences of the particular culture into which they are born and raised. His concept of the 'zone of proximal development' has been particularly significant in education. This concept represents the gap between what a child is capable of achieving with assistance and what can be achieved independently. These might be thought of as the 'buds' and the 'fruits' of development. It provides a valuable representation that has been used in constructing supportive learning environments featuring interaction and scaffolding.[10] In contrast to Piaget, Vygotsky believed it was the support and social interaction of the more competent other that led development. Consequently, the role of the 'expert other' in progressing learning within the child's zone of proximal development was seen as crucial; however, '*the child is not merely a passive recipient of adult guidance and assistance; in instructional programs, the active involvement of the child is crucial*'. Fundamentally Vygotsky believed that development was '*transformation through action*'.[11] This idea can be incorporated into a theory known as social constructivism. This theory suggests that intelligence builds through external and practical learning which is gradually internalised. These capabilities develop and are usually gradually internalised through collaboration with key people – either adults and sometimes other children. This cognitive development takes the child from the point of joint-regulation (we do it together) to self-regulation (I do it for myself). This view of social learning has been further extended and developed by Jerome Bruner and more recently Barbara Rogoff. Bruner introduced the notion of *readiness for learning* and the term *spiral curriculum*. He believed that any subject could be taught at any stage of development as long as it was presented in a way that was appropriate to the child's cognitive abilities, gradually building upon these abilities and expanding to the level of full understanding and mastery. As well as recognising the need for children to be actively involved in learning he considered the importance of motivation, recognising that '*ideally, interest in the subject matter is the best stimulus for learning*'.[12]

Consider then some of the strategies that you might use to support learning in your setting. You might include some direct teaching related to building knowledge or skills or you might need to give additional support to challenge a misconception: '*Do you think you're pedalling fast enough?*' '*Try putting your hands together to catch the ball*'. Your support may include this type of commentary: '*You're climbing really high, you must be able to see much more than me*'. This helps plant seeds of ideas in a child's mind and reinforces their possible next level of thinking. However it is a professional balancing act that requires in-depth knowledge of the children you are supporting. If we acknowledge that young children are 'capable from birth' then we must give them the time they need to work through problems and find solutions themselves. It is important that they know you are there to support, but the learning and discoveries should be led by them. Young children are natural explorers when given rich opportunities. I have witnessed first-hand how engaged and involved play and learning can be and how physically demanding it often is. In reality there is enormous variation both in the order and magnitude of young children's physical development based on their age, experience, cultural norms and the individual child's genes.

Preparing the environment

> [T]he physical development of babies and young children must be encouraged through the provision of opportunities for them to be active and interactive and improve their skills of coordination, control, manipulation and movement.[13]

Consider carefully the areas and opportunities available daily for your children. Can they mix things together, move things and act as scientists to dig, sieve, deconstruct and evaluate? Do you provide access to environments full of loose parts, both large and small, that empower creativity? What we sometimes call 'loose parts' can be natural or man-made, and most natural outdoor environments offer an abundance of loose parts for use in play; examples include:

- stumps, pallets, buckets and stones
- baskets, rope, crates and tyres
- boxes, shells, logs and pebbles
- sand, seedpods, gravel and leaves
- fabric, flowers, twigs, corks, feathers and grain.

These materials can be included and utilised inside and out, offering countless opportunities to transport, balance, combine, redesign, order and dismantle in multiple ways. They come with no specific set of instructions and can be used alone or combined with other materials, commonly found in early years settings, such as sand, blocks or incorporated into role play. These interesting, sensory items engage young minds and bodies in active explorations, often leading to those wonderful moments of awe and wonder that we all recognise.

Awe and wonder

As I observe a group of toddlers arriving at the nursery one morning my attention is drawn to a young child sitting on the carpet alone. He seems engrossed in his play, ignoring the other children and staff coming and going around him. As I move closer I can see that his attention is drawn by light shining through a stained-glass window at one end of the building. He is moving his hand in and out of the coloured lights as they merge together beneath him. He stands and enthusiastically moves his body, dancing in the midst of the colours, mesmerised by the experience. He brings his hands together as if cupping water, moving them upwards toward the source of the light. After several minutes of pirouetting and tiptoeing nearer and nearer to the window, the angle of the lights becomes too high for him to reach. He leaves the area and rummages over in the sand and water zone, returning with a bucket. This little scientist then attempts to collect the coloured lights in his bucket as if it were water. He persists for some time, gazing into the bucket as if expecting to find a captured treasure. His previous experiences with the properties of water and in particular the addition of colours to the water seemed to have led to these connections being formed. This active exploration led to an interest in light that was extended and developed over several months. It included experiences with the light tables, overhead projector, torches and dark room. Through active exploration and sensory experiences, multiple loose resources such as those described above were added to his environment to enable him to explore shadow, light, colours, reflection and refraction.

The diagram below outlines the important interaction of the child with the light from the stained-glass window (the mover), the environmental context and a movement task. It demonstrates the complex system of interactions between the child, the surroundings, the available resources and the cultural context.

The model in the diagram shows how each aspect of this interaction enables progress towards the child's goal.

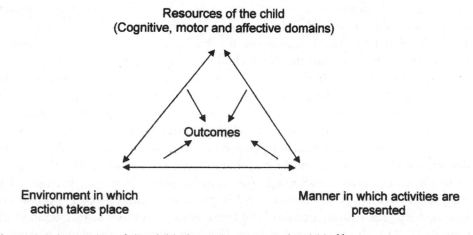

Figure 3.2 *Interaction of the child, the environment and activities*[14]

'The sand's here!'

It is easy to actively involve children in the day-to-day routines and jobs within a setting. Snack and meal times offer an abundance of opportunities for children to be engaged, developing their independence, their thinking skills and communication.

Recently, as spring approached and more children were playing and exploring in the construction area of the preschool garden, several children discovered that the sand pit was looking depleted and required re-filling. They eagerly communicated their findings back to an interested practitioner who listened to their suggestions, using the children's interest to make a list. With her pad and pen she noted down the children's request, then gave them a copy of the form, asking them to check it and sign for the order. One child suggested he knew where sand came from, naming the large supermarket nearby; his mum had already bought a bag for his sand pit at home. One child thought we could go to the nearby beach for some; he remarked that they have plenty there! Another said that on holiday the sand was black, but he wasn't sure why. What followed was a lengthy discussion between the practitioner and children related to quantity: how much sand did they think they needed? How much is in a bag anyway?

The children took the form and incorporated it within their play for about forty minutes, representing their sophisticated thinking with a variety of mathematical graphics and symbols. This activity led to further order forms and clip boards being added to the sand area over the following few days as an extension of this learning. Several days later a tonne bag of sand was delivered on a pallet into the children's garden. They watched in anticipation, excitedly shouting directions to the driver as the delivery arm hooked the bag of sand over the wall. The practitioners then asked any interested children how they thought the sand could be moved into the construction area as it was some distance from the delivery site. Their thoughts and ideas were noted on a mind map giving them opportunities to think, be creative and collaborate with others. Ideas were sparked from one child to another. All suggestions were acknowledged, and after collecting resources from around the nursery, the children set to work moving the sand. They used a variety of implements including spoons, buckets, spades and wheelbarrow to manoeuvre skilfully around the other children, emptying much of the sand from the bag into the brick-built sand pit. Any sand that was lost on the way was systematically swept up by another child who worked tirelessly with a broom and dustpan. The children had to work together, communicating and responding to each other; they showed persistence when the wheelbarrow became too heavy for them to push alone, requiring group effort to move it over a small step. They demonstrated team work, problem solving and determination and throughout were physically active, developing large muscle groups and core strength. This experience was led by the children and initiated by them; however the skill of a knowledgeable practitioner enabled the learning opportunities to be extended and supported. The children involved were highly motivated and gained a sense of achievement when others commented on how strong they were to move all that sand.Following the activity the practitioners decided, rather than buying grow bags for the garden this year, it would be more beneficial to have soil delivered in the same way, enabling the children to be actively involved in designing and establishing new growing areas.

Challenges and dilemmas

- Ensure adults are available to support and scaffold the children's learning as they play, encouraging collaboration and group work.
- Be aware of adults who may have a tendency to control learning, giving specific instructions and requiring set outcomes.
- Offer genuine encouragement when working with a child on a joint task.

- Developmental theories such as those of Piaget have been seen as linear, with children following similar pathways to adulthood. New theories assume that development proceeds in a web of multiple strands, with different children following different pathways.
- It is important to understand and accept that babies and young children are not simply onlookers and spectators of their social world; they are active contributors from birth.
- Active learners are questioners and inventors. How can you encourage the children in your care to hypothesise, '*I wonder how. . .?*'
- Active learning is an ongoing, inventive process in which children combine materials, experiences and ideas to produce effects that are new to them. Although adults may take for granted the laws of nature and logic, each child discovers them as if for the first time.

CHAPTER 4

Creating and thinking critically

Children want space at all ages. Space, that is ample space, is almost as much wanted as food and air. To move, to run, to find things out by new movement, to feel one's life in every limb, that is the life of early childhood.[1]

The 2012 Early Education Conference in Greenwich, 'Life in Every Limb', explored the need to promote physical development as a fundamental aspect of child development with passion and enthusiasm. This was in addition to the aim of raising well-being. The majority of early years practitioners and parents acknowledge the links between physical activity and health. However it is essential that we are all reminded of the importance of movement and physical development in terms of the environment, risk taking, imagination, creativity and the freedom that children need in order to move and express themselves. With creating and thinking critically identified in the new Early Years framework as a characteristic of effective teaching and learning, it is important for practitioners to consider the need for children to have and develop their own ideas, make connections and develop strategies to support their learning.

This chapter discusses how practitioners can support children to think creatively using their whole bodies, making reference to the movement play specialists JABADAO. This child-led movement play involving babies and young children makes a significant contribution to raising well-being in addition to supporting learning and development across all areas of the Early Years Foundation Stage. Children's critical thinking in relation to physical development involves their enjoyment in spontaneous movement; encouraging children to discover and explore their environment through physical encounters stimulates cognitive involvement.

The chapter will draw on the work of Montessori and the Reggio Emilia approach to early years education: that of valuing the environment and encouraging young children to engage physically with their world. Montessori recognised movement as a particularly sensitive aspect of a child's development, describing children's hands as '*the instruments of their brains*'. The more recent work of Sally Goddard Blythe describes movement as a child's first language and argues that young children '*learn with their bodies before they learn with their minds*'.[2] Goddard

Blythe recognises the importance of physical development from birth, proposing that children who experience an incomplete transition between the primary reflexes to early motor development can exhibit a number of later problems. She maintains that a healthy mind is created by the brain and the body operating together in harmony, and that this requires repeated physical experiences. Movement therefore is both the primary motivator and medium through which learning and brain development takes place.

Early movement and tummy time

With almost half of babies in the UK now being cared for outside the home, it is imperative to start our discussion of movement play from an early age. Babies' early movements, such as stretching, kicking and crawling, are essential for their development because they help to establish and develop neural pathways in the brain. Research has now suggested that some young children who have started to walk very early may be missing the crawling stage which has now been recognised as establishing the foundations for many later important skills. Research by Goddard Blythe (co-director of the Institute for Neuro-Physiological Psychology), working with groups of children in primary schools who are experiencing a range of difficulties, suggests that *'early walkers have a hyper-advanced sense of balance but lack skills such as concentration and sitting still'*.[3] She repeatedly promotes the need for babies during their first year to have regular opportunities for 'tummy time' on the floor. The significance of a baby's rapid physical development has important implications for good practice in childcare settings. The Babyroom Project, led by Dr Kathy Goouch and Dr Sacha Powell of Canterbury Christ Church University, reported that often staff working in baby rooms, although committed to their roles, were less qualified and attended fewer training courses than other staff within a nursery setting. It is important to recognise that knowledgeable staff are the most important resource in a setting. The UK Physical Activity Guidelines (2011) developed by the British Heart Foundation promote unrestricted floor-based activities and regular opportunities for tummy time. Sally Goddard Blythe says of the floor that:

> It is the best playground of all for babies – forget expensive toys and equipment, babies need to be given the opportunity to develop the strength of body control for themselves. Through tummy time, children learn to hold their neck up and strengthen their shoulders and upper body. I call this the putting in of vocabulary of movement, which supports the very many later functions such as good posture, balance and hand-eye co-ordination.[4]

In tummy time a baby learns:

- to turn and lift their head
- to hand grip
- control of the upper body

- to roll over
- to strengthen the back and the arms.

So to summarise: the more free movement babies have on their tummies, the greater the brain development.

By being positioned regularly on their stomach, babies develop the physical strength and muscle tone to then start to crawl. Crawling has now been accepted as vitally important for the wiring in the brain, in particular to develop the cross-pattern movements of the arms and legs. Each movement of the arm or leg creates a signal to the motor cortex of the brain so the more the opportunities to repeat these actions and in turn fire these signals, the stronger the connections in the brain and the more fluid the movement becomes. Some older children in primary schools are being returned to these primitive movements in order to establish missing connections. Proprioception, the understanding of where your body is in space, is developed by these early messages from the tactile input of the ground and the feeling each movement creates. Thus the child establishes that they have to coordinate the movements of each limb and develop an understanding of the relationship between their two legs, two arms, two feet and two hands as they move these against the floor.

Crawling engages almost all the major muscles of the body, from the arches of the feet to the stomach and neck muscles, all of which are combined in the process of moving the body forwards. Arm, back and chest muscles are employed in pulling the arms forward and thus pulling the body forward; quads, hips and hamstrings are worked as part of the leg movements. For the child this is a full body workout, but more importantly it establishes important neural connections that integrate sensory input. The repeated movements of crawling provide the brain with what some have argued is the best integrated sensory input, sending simultaneous information to the brain from both the tactile and proprioceptive receptors, the surface receptors, the deep receptors and the proprioceptive receptors in the joints. In addition, the brain is receiving simultaneous input from the coordinated movement of the right arm and left leg, and the left arm and right leg. However, it must be noted that children who walk much earlier may return to crawling movements later on and should be encouraged to do so.

Crawling

Crawling helps a child's development in the following ways:

- by the integration of the two halves of the brain's motor cortex – the 'mind/body' connection
- by encouraging true creativity; understanding and learning occur when the left (logic) hemisphere of the brain and the right (global) hemisphere are used together
- by the strengthening of legs and limbs and developing hand and eye coordination

- by helping the understanding that we have two sides of the body and how to use and coordinate them
- by encouraging balance in movementby encouraging spatial awareness, which if not learned properly can cause problems such as clumsiness, being slow to learn left and right, reversal of letters when reading and writing, and movement challenges such as balancing and spinning.

Figure 4.1 *The mind/body connection*

Consider a baby at birth, unable to control movements, yet less than a year later many babies are starting to take their first steps. This desire to walk is instinctive and requires little teaching or coaching; in fact most young toddlers will become extremely upset if these needs are obstructed, albeit by a well-meaning adult. Think about the frustrated toddler fighting to get out of your arms in order to return to his endeavours. For the young child this is conscious work, requiring repeated rehearsal and practice as their movements become extended and their balance is adjusted. Through her many observations of babies and young children Montessori recognised that they were always moving, exploring with their senses using hands, mouth, eyes and ears. She advocated free movement as *'being able to move one's body without artificial aids, to be able to move according to developing abilities, gradually learning to reach and to grasp, to turn over, to crawl, to sit up, and to pull oneself up to a standing position and walk; all on one's own'.*[5] Montessori believed that by carefully preparing the environment, adults could support children and help them to develop through motor activity. Her emphasis on developing independence and self-reliance was reinforced by her belief in the sensitivity of young children to movement. This recognition that young children had an inbuilt desire to move in order to learn is now clearly supported by more recent advances in brain imaging and neuroscience.

As babies grow into toddlers one of the recognised interests that they show is that of climbing. Once they are established walkers, able to negotiate toys, furniture and other children with ease, often carrying a multitude of items with them, their attention turns to the other components in the room. Anything that can be climbed on will be considered fair game, including the furniture, resources and the staff. Practitioners need to be aware of the potential dangers of this new development but, as much as possible, their role here should be to facilitate. As with all physical skills the children will repeat the process over and over, often seeking a more challenging climb. In the home setting, of course, this requires stair gates to be fitted as a flight of stairs offers real dangers for these young climbers. However, staff teams need to meet and discuss how the environments for these children can enable and support this development rather than close it down.

'Everybody needs to play': the work of JABADAO

JABADAO, the National Centre for Movement, Learning and Health, was set up by dancers some twenty-five years ago to work with those involved in group care. This includes early years settings, schools, the elderly and patients with dementia. In the developmental movement for the early years, a programme of play was devised in order to change the way early years practitioners and parents support young children's physicality. In 1998 JABADAO set up an independent action research project to find and test an effective way to improve the confidence among early years practitioners, running movement activities with babies and young children. In discussion with practitioners across twenty-six settings the results suggested that staff felt they lacked the training required to understand physical development in young children. Working today, the organisation continues to enhance understanding of movement and brain development for practitioners, parents, children's centres and childminders. One of the more recent programmes 'Dad the Human Play Frame' was devised to encourage fathers to become more involved in vigorous movement play such as throwing children in the air and catching them or spinning around with them. Interestingly in the research project it was reported that children were most drawn to movement play that involved 'spin-tip-roll-fall'. These were fun activities with some challenge that generally involved rocking, balance, swinging, tilting and rotation and help strengthen immature neuromotor skills.

Key aspects of the work of JABADAO:

- Movement is not based within a performance tradition but on everyday life.
- It helps children learn to be comfortable in their own skin.
- It is spontaneous, improvised, created in the moment.
- It is about the feeling of movement, the feeling of being 'me'.

- It supports the human need to move in ways for which our physiology has developed.
- It delights in exuberance and playfulness.
- Movement is created and re-created, as a collective endeavour, by those involved.
- It encourages spontaneous responses (improvisation) rather than rehearsed pieces.[6]

Penny Greenland, director of JABADAO, argues that it is not helpful for young children to be kept restricted in prams or seats for long periods of time. '*Small children move all the time because they are responding to a biological drive to develop well. Missing out early movement play is like missing out the foundations of a house; you never know what cracks and problems may appear later on.*'

I often hear practitioners discussing practice within their own setting and it would appear that babies and toddlers in particular are restricted in terms of what they can do to further their physical development; either due to fears of safety or because of routines in the settings. They may go for walks, but are not allowed out of the pushchairs or they may spend much of their day either strapped into a swing, chair or walker. They are limited to small enclosed spaces in which to explore. Rather than propping babies upright before they have developed the core strength to support themselves, or using artificial walking aids, it may be better for adults to lay down with the babies and join in with their tummy time. After all it's a workout for your body as well as theirs!

So be creative with your space, get down to the children's level and ask yourself, for whom is the environment created, and how often is the space changed to add interest, challenge and opportunities? Seek exciting outdoor natural spaces for your children that enable them to become actively involved and engaged. Shirley Brice Heath argues passionately that childhood today has, for many children, simply become a prolonged period of '*spectatorship learning*'.[7] She argues that young children now often wait to be entertained by others, missing out entirely on the learning that comes from '*direct experiences, participation and collaboration*'. Concerns are growing worldwide about the reduction of time young children spend outdoors in freely chosen play activities. It appears that this time is gradually being replaced by new exciting digital entertainment, with some children spending up to eight hours a day as passive spectators rather than active participants. The National Trust has become so concerned about some aspects of childhood that it launched a new campaign in 2011 to get the UK's 'cotton wool kids' outdoors. The top twenty activities listed can easily be adapted and developed for very young children and provide ample opportunities for children to develop and refine their physical skills, imagination and creativity:

- climb a tree
- roll down a really big hill
- camp out in the wild
- build a den
- skim a stone

- run around in the rain
- fly a kite
- catch a fish with a net
- eat an apple straight from a tree
- play with conkers
- throw some snow
- hunt for treasure on the beach
- make a mud pie
- dam a stream
- go sledging
- bury someone in the sand
- set up a snail race
- balance on a fallen tree
- swing on a rope swing
- make a mud slide.[8]

Lessons from Reggio Emilia

Case study: Walkergate Early Years Centre

The Sightlines Initiative is an organisation that promotes creative and reflective practice in early childhood education. It is the United Kingdom reference for and link to the preschools of Reggio Emilia. The Sightlines Initiative worked with the setting to create *The Creative Thinking in Action Project: Death, Fear and Bravado.* This short case study formed part of a larger project that culminated with the production of the 'Experiments and Encounters' exhibit.

The children's journey begins following an observed interest in dancing amongst the group. The staff at the setting make every effort to support this, forming a special 'dancing room' indoors that incorporates music and natural materials as a stimulus for movement. The children skip about the room but it appears as if the dance is more a performance for the adults and each other rather than an expressive language of movement. With an understanding of the children and their interests, the staff team discuss what intervention, if any, is appropriate. They want to develop the children's natural creativity and expressive movement so decide to offer the group the stimulus of a visit to a beach. During the visit the children explore the sand, sea, rocks and caves:

'*Go on, I've been in the cave, I want to climb those rocks.*'

The children then find a dead fish and a bird's foot:

'*Look, a foot, a foot! Look at this foot.*'
Amy: '*Did you touch it?*' (She studies the foot carefully.)
Adam: '*I touched it.*'
Darius: '*Ah, I can see its teeth.*' The children all want to touch the eye of the fish.

The children collect all sorts of treasures and bring them back to the nursery where they are examined and displayed. Some children look at items on the light table.

> Adam (looking at the dried-up seaweed): '*It's died like the fish.*'
> The children submerge the dried weed in water and watch it come back to life.
> Adam: '*If we put the fish back in the water would that come alive?*'

The children then use the visit to the beach to inspire their interest in movement and dance. They move naturally to the music, without inhibition, seeming to conjure their dance from inside them. This level of creativity requires a special kind of secure, respectful environment. So have their experiences on the beach radically altered their movement repertoire? A member of staff, who worked with the children, said:

> You could see, there really was a connection between the movement and the experiences at the beach. It was dramatic, this sudden change, and they just moved in a completely different way after the experience. They were really talking. They kept looking back at the trough and touching the things in the trough. All their senses brought them to that state.

The skipping has disappeared and is replaced by an astonishing performance. The staff analyse the movements and responses by the children and decide to offer them another experience of sea creatures up close and moving. They arrange a visit to a marine centre and take along a professional dancer who could support the children's ideas. The centre is close to the beach they had previously visited so they return to the sand with materials brought from the nursery. This time the dance reveals a powerful connection between their ideas of the creatures and their physicality. Using the red cloth as a train, the children return to the caves full of stories from their previous visit. Again there are monsters and elements of apprehension, boldness and curiosity.

The following week the dancer works with the children drawing directly from their experiences at the beach. The dancer intervenes to introduce a new movement vocabulary to the children. They explore jumping, spinning, rolling, fast, slow, and being statues, using props such as floaty scarves, stretchy elastic and large birth balls. Each brings its own quality of movement to the children's dance. They incorporate shadow play, an assortment of different music, take photographs of each other dancing and use paint to capture marks made as they dance.

The final stage of the project was a mixture of dance, paint and recollection, which allowed the children to look back at images of the objects collected on the beach and paint their own interpretations on silk. This creative, multi-layered approach to practice allows children, practitioners and parents to work together as co-researchers without a focused outcome in mind. The use of the beach environment close to the setting stimulated thinking, talk and action and provided the active physical aspects of deep-level learning. Children were allowed time to reflect and explore without unnecessary interruption and their involvement and flow in the ideas generated were contagious. The dancer and staff enabled the children's development *'allowing the physical to come first...encouraging the boys with physical play and drawing out other ideas with them'.*[9]

Some might argue that taking young children out of the safety of the early years setting is fraught with difficulty. I agree it takes organisation and planning; however, just because something is difficult it should not prevent us from doing it. Organisations such as the National Children's Bureau have questioned the 'richness' of creative experiences currently experienced by England's youngest children when compared to other European countries. The government has made it clear that we cannot *'wrap our children up in cotton wool... we should recognise that it can be a terrifically fortifying experience, arming young children with the resilience, robustness and creativity they will need to deal with the challenges of the big wide world.'*[10] What can we learn from creative examples of this kind?

Key messages for practice include:

- the importance of the environment both in and around the setting
- a positive acknowledgement that children's natural enthusiasm and curiosity can lead learning
- all learning involves elements of creativity
- adults need to take children's ideas seriously
- children need to take risks and be challenged
- time for reflection and discussion of next steps is crucial
- children must be supported to make meaning from their experiences
- encouraging children to use all their senses deepens learning
- stand back to see what intrigues, inspires and tests children
- when planning a project, discuss a range of representation, including images and symbols
- promote possibility thinking (what is...to what might be)
- promote the development of children's imagination
- listen and respond to children's questions
- document the learning to make it visual
- allow children to revisit ideas
- time is as long as it takes.

The Montessori approach

Montessori's belief in the prepared environment for young children is echoed in the Reggio Emilia preschools in Northern Italy where it is suggested that the environment is the third teacher. Here babies and young children are seen as rich and capable with the potential to lead learning. The centres provide environments that are carefully planned and organised, cultivating the disposition for creativity and critical thinking to develop. This focus on the environment led Montessori to describe it as 'calling' to the children, actively encouraging interest and involvement.

Practitioners are part of the learning environment, and just as we have a responsibility to offer wonderful sights, textures, sounds, tastes and smells for children we also have a responsibility to provide enriching movement experiences. Baroness Susan Greenfield from Oxford University suggests that the human brain, in comparison to those of other species, is highly responsive and malleable. She describes the environment as the key to everything. It is therefore crucial for anyone working with young children to understand how very sensitive young children's brains are, and how they can be shaped and changed by the potentials of the environment.

Challenges and dilemmas

Consider the extent of movement play within young children's daily lives. Research shows that movement prompts development of both the body and the brain. If we miss out on movement play as children, it can have significant effects on the rest of our lives. Think about the challenges, opportunities and physical needs of these children. Look at your space from the child's viewpoint and consider:

- Is there ample space for children to move freely throughout the day?
- Do you have areas that link movement with music, light or water?
- Can children create their own environments, inside and out?
- Do you encourage regular tummy time for babies and games that involve crawling?
- Can babies crawl outside across a range of different surfaces?
- Are there regular opportunities for young children to remove socks and shoes, to feel natural textures underfoot?
- Do you plan activities that encourage children to be creative with their whole bodies?
- Can furniture and fittings be moved and rearranged as children's physical skills develop? Can you create obstacle courses and take items from the inside to the outside?
- Do you facilitate challenges such as steps, stairs and slopes?
- Can children use real tools in order to gain mastery, control and independence?
- Have you included a digging area within your outdoor space?
- Can children safely swing upside down from a tyre, rope or branch?
- Do you provide opportunities for children approaching three to use 'maximum effort' to develop stamina such as going for long walks?
- Are children always grouped by age or can they spend some time with older children?
- Do you consider your environment in terms of a shop window, i.e. rich in possibilities?
- Are provocations and loose parts included regularly to challenge thinking? (Loose parts are items other than toys such as scrap, like scaffold boards, guttering and tubes. They are provided to encourage children to think and to provoke an interest)

- What opportunities are there to develop balance and coordination?
- Are children encouraged to help with daily routines, washing up, sweeping floors?
- How is your environment set up for children with limited mobility?
- How much time do young children spend restricted in chairs, prams or walkers?
- Is the environment prepared to offer some rest and relaxation?
- Can babies and young children safely sleep outside?

CHAPTER 5

Building developing competence

One of the greatest mistakes of our day is to think of movement by itself, as something apart from the higher functions. We think of our muscles as organs to be used only for health purposes. We 'take exercise' or do gymnastics, to keep ourselves 'fit' to make us breathe, eat or sleep better. It is an error which has been taken over by the schools... But to be always thinking of the mind, on one hand, and the body, on the other, is to break the continuity that should reign between them.[1]

Those of us who work closely with young children and families understand the growing importance of movement in relation to health, education and well-being. It's not surprising, however, that parents and practitioners are pushed towards the false notion that the mind and body are separate and the functions of the mind are superior to those of the body. Many believe that children routinely acquire and perfect motor skills, such as walking, running and balancing, believing it to be a natural maturation process for all children. This may largely be true but it is only part of the process. Many children are entering compulsory schooling without the fully developed physical skills that might be expected for their age. This can be seen in the difficulties they experience with balance, coordination, fine motor skills, concentration and posture. The initial primitive reflexes present at birth, which are discussed in detail below, need to be gradually inhibited in the first year in order to adapt into more mature postural reflexes by the time a child is three and a half. Children with limited experiences of essential movements can be negatively affected, resulting in immature neuro-motor skills which, in turn, might lead to them having significant difficulties and underachieving at school. It is important, therefore, that practitioners have a basic knowledge of these reflexes so that they can provide the best possible environment which will support children's physical development as they mature.

Development from birth: the 'primitive reflexes'

Physical development starts at birth with the progressive inhibition of the primitive reflexes that all humans are born with. In order for future development to occur, the brain needs to take over these functions so the reflex becomes a brain function rather than a reflex. This is inhibition. These reflexes checked at, or soon after birth, by a health visitor, are indicators of healthy development in-vitro, but as the baby grows and develops, it is the inhibition of these reflexes which allows for the progressive development of new physical skills linked to both their gross and fine motor skills: those of crawling, walking, balancing, coordination and communication. Children who retain one or more of these primitive reflexes may present a number of developmental delays and disorders. These, then, are the primitive reflexes and how they affect physical development.

The Moro reflex

The Moro, or startle, reflex is present at birth and is usually inhibited between two and four months. This is the baby's response to potential danger, such as being dropped or hearing a loud noise. It is experienced by a baby as physical stress and triggers chemical releases in the brain such as adrenaline and cortisol. Imagine throwing a very young baby into the air and catching them in the same way as an older toddler. The squeals of joy heard from a toddler would be replaced with screams of alarm. The resulting cries and movement of the limbs when the head is gently dropped back indicate healthy development particularly in relation to the spinal cord. However, if the reflex is retained, even partially, the baby will be oversensitive and reactive to light, noise, movement and may appear on edge. Later on in their childhood these children often are seen to dislike rough and tumble play, are sensitive to wind or rain in their faces, often observe rather than joining in with others and can be hypersensitive to sound, light and texture.

The grasping reflex

The grasping reflexes usually develop and inhibit at roughly the same time as the Moro reflex, and can be divided into the *palmar*, *plantar*, *rooting* and *infantile suck reflexes*. Again they are related to survival and the need to suckle.

The palmar reflex

This is noticeable at birth when anything placed in the baby's palm is automatically grasped. The responding movement and grasp of the fingers over the thumb is strong and can take time to relax.

The plantar reflex

The plantar reflex is in essence a very similar reaction but seen in the baby's foot. Any stimulation of the foot results in the curling of the toes and flexing of the arch, taking the heel toward the ball of the foot.

The rooting reflex

This is seen in very young babies, with a reaction to a stimulus on the cheek resulting in the head turning towards what they perceive as a food source and an automatic search for the nipple. Related to the baby's need for nourishment, the infantile suck reflex is the sucking response at the front of the mouth involving the lips, jaw and tongue. This is completely different to the adult sucking reaction, which involves the tongue moving against the palate at the rear of the mouth.

If these primitive grasping reflexes are not fully inhibited during babyhood the resulting difficulties for an infant can include:

- poor control of cutlery when eating, leading to prolonged messy eating
- a tendency to suck food rather than chew it, poor saliva control and excessive dribbling
- sensitivity in and around the mouth; they can be very fussy eaters
- poor control of the mouth for speech which may require speech therapy
- reduced running skills, more tripping and falling
- some noticeable difficulty with fine motor control and difficulty with pincer grip
- difficulties with bladder control.

Asymmetrical tonic neck reflex

The function of this primitive reflex is to slow down and assist in the birth process, to initiate outer limb movement and start hand–eye coordination. It is activated by the labyrinth in the inner ear and results in asymmetrical movements of the limbs in response to movements of the head. The reflex is usually inhibited at about six months so that focus on distant objects can be developed, but is evident as babies start to roll over as they will be seen to focus on near and far objects. It is this primitive reflex that enables humans to make the cross–over movements; essential for crawling and later marching using alternate leg and arm movements. If the ATNR is not fully inhibited the child may exhibit:

- poor writing and difficulty in copying, tight pencil grip, often experiencing writer's cramp with extended writing
- difficulties with reading or following a line of text, often gets lost on the page or loses their place. There can be a reversal of letters and numbers and poor knowledge of right and left
- reduced hand–eye coordination and difficulties with balance.

Tonic labyrinthine reflex

The TLR or tonic labyrinthine reflex is fully present at birth and is related to the tilting of the head forwards and backwards. It is closely linked to the Moro reflex both being vestibular in origin and activated by movements of the head (see Chapter 8). This reflex is seen when a baby is lying on its front. It will automatically adopt a curled-up position. Alternatively, when the head is tilted backwards the muscles on the back of the body and limbs contract resulting in babies extending their arms and legs and arching their back. Usually inhibited by four months, any retained reflex can lead to difficulties with motion sickness, spatial problems, poor posture and muscle tone, poor sequencing skills, a range of visual perceptual difficulties and a poor sense of time. In terms of physical development they may dislike their arms being above their head, swinging or climbing a rope, may have some fear of height and difficulties with perception, often banging into things or knocking them over.

Symmetrical tonic neck reflex

The symmetrical tonic neck reflex (flexion and extension) is not present at birth but develops when a baby is between six to nine months old and is inhibited at around nine to eleven months. The STNR precedes the ability to crawl and this reflex enables the child to move onto its knees, either adopting a crawl or standing position. The reflex allows the eyes to make adjustments from near to far vision during this stage, as the eyes are lowered to the floor or raised to view the play space. Again incomplete inhibition can negatively affect posture and hand-eye coordination.

Developing all the senses

In her book *Sensory Integration and the Child,* Jean Ayres describes the importance of physical activities for young children as *'food for the brain'.*[2] She maintains that it is our senses that provide the knowledge needed to inform and direct the body and mind, but that it is the brain which must organise and understand these messages. Although we are all familiar with the senses involved in taste, sight, smell and sound and touch, many of us do not realise the importance of these other senses relating to movement, force of gravity, and body position.

Although human development is rich, diverse, and enormously complex, the sequence of motor development in young babies and children follows a similar pattern; however, what varies from individual to individual is the rate of growth. This rate of growth is dependent on a complex synthesis of genes and environmental stimuli. Evidence drawn from a range of disciplines suggests that meeting the developmental needs of young children is as much about building a strong foundation for life-long physical and mental health as it is about enhancing readiness to succeed in school.[3] Some have compared a child's developing health and physical skills in the early years to the launching of a rocket, suggesting that it is the minor difficulties that emerge shortly after take-off that have the most significant effect on its ultimate trajectory.[4]

Early milestones

The literature review which informed the new EYFS is based on the important work of Maude, Chambers and Sugden. They outline two key processes that appear to order the sequence of physical development in infants.[5] The first is cephalo-caudal development, described as the 'top-downwards' development; that is, from the head down to the feet. This is observed as babies begin to increasingly develop some control over their bodies, first with head movements, then, as the primitive reflexes are inhibited, taking control of first their arms then their legs. This process of development is seen as babies learn to control their upper body. A baby sitting with support and with activities to hand, such as interest baskets or treasure baskets, is encouraged in their hand-eye coordination, balance and visual perception.

A baby's physical development can be rapid and change almost weekly, from them lying seemingly helpless to gradually rolling, sitting, crawling, standing and eventually walking. Proximo-distal development, the second type suggested by Maude, Chambers and Sugden, is described in the literature review as '*development proceeding from the centre of the body outwards. This is related to the development of the central nervous system and its relationship with the major organs found in the centre of the body.*' This gradual motor development can be seen from the seemingly indiscriminate waving of the arms or legs in early infancy, to the later controlled use of the shoulders, knees, elbows, hands, feet and fingers.

Within the setting, mealtimes offer great opportunities to develop motor skills, and provide a time to observe any difficulties that children with some retention of primitive reflexes may have. The most recent research by Gill Rapley[6] suggests babies begin to reach for food at around six months, which is around the time now recommended by health visitors, in accordance with the World Health Organisation guidelines. This baby-led weaning cuts out the need for pureed food and introduces babies to whole food straight away. Starting in this way with a small range of finger foods strengthens both hand-eye coordination and the muscles of the mouth, lips and jaw.[7]

Moving on to using a bowl and spoon at mealtimes offers further opportunities to develop physical skills. As well as coordinating hand and mouth movements, the young child has to use complex physical control to first gather some food then carefully balance the spoon from the bowl to the mouth. The movements require concentration, upper body strength, posture, coordination and motor skills, in addition to differentiation, i.e., the ability of the child to judge the distance and alter the position of the arm using the elbow joint with skill and ease. However challenging and messy this may appear for young children, they are motivated to keep trying. It is our responsibility to support them and nurture these key experiences rather than simply seeing them as daily routines that need to be rushed through as quickly as possible.

The importance of physical development as a prime area of learning

A key change in the new Early Years Foundation Stage is the distinction made between the prime and specific areas of learning. This focus on the three prime developmental areas – personal, social and emotional; physical; and speech and language – should encourage each of us working with the youngest children to reflect on our existing knowledge of child development and raise questions and discussions in relation to the opportunities we provide for them. Providing a strong developmental start in the early years increases the probability of positive outcomes in later life. Conversely, and possibly more importantly, a weak foundation significantly increases the risk of later difficulties.[8] In terms of school readiness, young children in the Foundation years need daily opportunities to develop their whole bodies. These experiences are essential for developing core strength that in turn supports the development of the brain and central nervous system.

The new EYFS framework has given practitioners an opportunity to review their current understanding and knowledge in relation to child development. The distinction now being made between the prime and specific areas of learning should prompt enthusiastic discussions as staff teams meet together to plan, implement and discuss the implications for current practice. The three key differences between the prime and the specific areas of learning as set out in the Early Years framework were identified by Tickell in her independent report *Foundations for Life, Health and Learning*.[9] First, she acknowledges that the prime areas are time sensitive, a sentiment echoed in the work of Dr Montessori who described periods of early childhood as 'critical periods' for development. As such, if these areas are not firmly established by the age of five, they may hold the child back and it will be much more difficult for them to acquire these skills later in life. Second, it is acknowledged that the prime areas are universal, as they are the essential building blocks across socio-cultural contexts. Finally, it is recognised that the prime areas provide the context for all other areas of learning and should therefore be at the forefront when planning activities or implementing changes.

Between the ages of two and five, young children start to develop their fine motor skills. These skills can be strengthened by allowing children the time to dress themselves independently, gradually learning such skills as doing up buttons, putting on their own shoes and also starting to use cutlery to eat at the table. However these skills, like everything else, need lots of practice and adults have to be there to support and help but also to promote a sense of independence. The more we do things for young children the more we deny them the ability to develop for themselves. Montessori recognised this over a hundred years ago and developed furniture, tools and resources for young children which were designed to promote independence, autonomy and *practical life skills*. The activities in these practical life skills have a strong fine motor component and are invaluable in developing and extending children's fine motor abilities as well as their cognitive development. They promote pouring, folding, polishing and manipulation of interesting real objects including padlocks with keys, nuts and bolts, boxes with lids, jars with screw-top lids, different types of door locks, and bolts to remove with a tool.[10]

Figure 5.1 *Practical life skills*

Penny Greenland, director of JABADAO, the National Centre for Movement, Learning and Health, reminds us that

> Learning doesn't happen in neat hierarchical stages – just because we can walk doesn't mean we don't still need to spend time on the floor rolling, crawling and playing on our tummies...even when adults give children huge amounts of encouragement, they can still miss out areas of development at the textbook time, but then return to them later... Children need to be fully physical in all they do. It is not naughty or wilful; it's what their body needs.[11]

Finding their feet

Chambers and Sugden suggest that, for young toddlers, the process of walking becomes more natural after the age of two, recommending opportunities for them to walk at varying paces over different surfaces including slopes and uneven terrain. One of my clearest memories from childhood is the feeling of walking over the ridges in the sand left as the tide went out. These were natural contours created by the sea that were only present in the damp sand closest to the shore. Natural outdoor spaces provide an abundance of different experiences for young children; think about the physical differences and sensory experiences of walking over or through:

> long grass / wet grass / cut grass / straw / puddles
> sand dunes / wet sand / rock pools / seashore
> wood chippings / gravel / paving / stepping stones
> cobbles / slate / tiles / decking / woodland / mud

These changes in environments enable children to begin to vary their walking, strengthening the muscles in their legs and using different parts of their foot. The practitioner may encourage children to use a tiptoe action, stamp, walk backwards or indeed march using the cross-over movements of alternate legs and arms. Taking out instruments, drums or music to encourage the marching to a beat adds an extra dimension. As walking becomes more automatic and the young child is no longer having to think through each movement (much like an adult learning to drive a car), the movements become more stable and they then demonstrate their ability to multi-task, carrying around or moving objects. Again, much like an adult learning to drive, once the skill of driving is established, the process becomes automatic and thinking turns to planning dinner or the next meeting while driving to work.

Another significant development that follows in the preschool years is the young child's ability to learn to run. Chambers and Sugden[12] note that children begin to run at about eighteen months and that most toddlers are running around by the age of two. They acknowledge that strength and balance are essential components as running requires both legs to be lifted off the ground simultaneously and the child must then regain balance of their body after each step. However, by the age of four, most children can run confidently across and around other children, taking part in negotiating games with rules and complex movements.

Physical patterns of play

> Children learn best through physical and mental challenges. Active learning involves other people, objects, ideas and events that engage and involve children for sustained periods.[13]

The Practice Guidance for the Early Years Foundation Stage makes clear links between schemas or patterns of play and child development and recommends that practitioners should '*encourage young children as they explore particular patterns of thought or movement, sometimes referred to as schemas*'.[14] When these patterns of behaviour in young children's play are followed, the same actions are often uncovered that can lead to more interesting and motivating planning. Many recognised schemas involve physical skills such as jumping, throwing, moving and transporting. By incorporating these interests into daily experiences a good practitioner will see repeated opportunities for development and include them in their planning. In fact the EYFS reminds practitioners that it is the daily observations of what children do that will most significantly inform planning and provision: '*No plan written weeks in advance can include a child's interest in transporting small objects in a favourite blue bucket.*' Practitioners therefore need to be aware of children's schematic interests.

Two observations of play patterns

Daniel (fourteen months) and Ben (thirty-six months) have both been observed regularly with a noticeable trajectory schema. Daniel is extremely active, recently choosing to spend a great deal of his time throwing things. His key person also noted that during time in the garden he was particularly drawn to the straight lines of cement between the bricks of the garden wall. When offered water and a paint-brush he attempted to paint the horizontal lines in the brickwork. The movement of his body down the slide also seems to fascinate him and he repeated the action over and over again, running excitedly back to the steps to climb again.

Ben, who is also very lively, particularly enjoys repeatedly going up and down the climbing frame. He will often be found dressed as a superhero, jumping off the top, or balancing guttering or pipes from the top in order to post down his numerous superhero action figures, or cars, one by one. He demonstrates consid-erable agility and seems particularly interested in speed and height.

Although both boys are demonstrating a trajectory schema, their different ages and the accompanying understanding lead to different learning opportunities that can equally be supported and extended. Daniel is currently exploring an under-standing of up and down, while Ben is more advanced in his thinking, learning more about distance, speed and height.

Knowledgeable practitioners could use these observations of what children do to plan further opportunities to:

- explore movement and games outdoors that involve throwing for a purpose; for example using skittles, boules and beanbags
- encourage children to move their bodies over, under, across and through things, including scrap items such as tyres, planks, logs and scramble nets
- investigate alternate resources and equipment within the community – trampo-lines, swings or larger slides that are possibly available in a nearby park
- discuss interests and patterns of a child's behaviour with their parents so that they can support and understand their child's interest at home.

Amy and Christopher are older, aged forty-eight and thirty-six months respec-tively. They are both captivated by items that they can connect. Amy is often seen spending time at the craft table, creating objects with string, sellotape and the stapler. She is fascinated by what happens when she connects a variety of different objects and materials. These included creating a magnificent spider's web made of string that was tied between a number of chairs.

Christopher is more regularly observed outside, transporting guttering, planks and tubes that he connects to form complex structures. He is also particularly interested in the pulley in the sand pit. He is often seen transporting buckets of water to his structures and repeatedly travelling backwards and forwards to the tap, collecting water to test his construction. His play demonstrates a cluster of schemas and indicates an interest in science, cause and effect and logical thinking.

Both of these children have taken part in regular Forest School sessions and their ideas have been extended and built on using their interests in connecting things.

With the whole group, practitioners have planned opportunities to develop physical skills in addition to building relationships with others. They are using team games which include problem-solving activities where children work together to move themselves and their group across a ditch or stream. It involves using large loose parts such as tyres, planks and rope to construct a bridge that will safely allow the children to cross. Planned activities such as these allow the children to consolidate both knowledge and concepts, test theories and learn to manage larger tools and resources safely and in new ways. It is important to acknowledge the practitioner's key role here in creating a learning environment that is rich in resources and materials, and purposefully supports the development of ideas, thus engaging with children to scaffold and extend their learning.

This chapter has considered the EYFS requirement to now focus on the importance of the three prime areas of learning and development. Supporting children through daily routines and planning activities that follow their interests and promote independence lead to dynamic play environments that offer multiple opportunities for physical development. With a renewed focus on the health and physical capabilities of young children, practitioners must rethink practice and reflect on their current understanding to support this. As Mordy and Hess said almost fifty years ago:

> physical education is about developing an understanding of self, the environmental and social factors which influence movement and an appreciation of how physical activity contributes to well being.[15]

Challenges and dilemmas

- How can children's patterns of play lead planning for physical development?
- How much open space do you provide in rooms for young children to move freely? Can you remove some furniture or resources to create more space?
- Once walking, can groups of young children visit natural environments that offer a variety of terrains underfoot? Remember these opportunities change with the weather.
- Is there space outdoors for running games that incorporate stop and go? It is important for young children to learn how to stop as well as having the independence and space to run freely.
- How are the key messages relating to the importance of physical development shared with parents? Can you engage parents in more conversations related to health and especially exercise?
- What support or help can other professionals or organisations locally offer your setting in terms of improving physical development and health?

CHAPTER 6

Engaging families

Whatever their specialism, practitioners in the foundation years have a common commitment to children's healthy growth and development and working with their families. Making this goal a reality requires motivated, qualified, and confident leaders and professionals across health, early years and social care committed to working closely together in the interests of children and families.[1]

It has been a privilege to have been part of the early years workforce for over twenty-five years and a parent for almost thirty. During this time of rapid changes I have witnessed first-hand the positive influences that knowledgeable early years practitioners can make across a range of settings and children's centres. Parenting, too, has always been full of challenges; I remember vividly the experience of becoming a mother, suddenly having the responsibility of this new life. With the support of an extended family close by I rapidly learnt which of my daughter's cries meant she was hungry and that she enjoyed kicking on her mat without a nappy. I became a regular face at the clinic and toddler group making many new friends who became my sounding board; supporting and guiding all manner of questions relating to breastfeeding, weaning, sleeping, walking and my anxieties relating to my child's lack of speech. This 'community of learners', as I now see it, discussed, reflected, hypothesised and supported my new-found interest in child development.

I believe today that many parents share my interest and desire to understand and provide the best opportunities for their children. However, it would appear that families in general are facing increased pressures, leading to parents very often feeling overwhelmed or unprepared for the responsibilities and constant changes that young children bring. We must remember that parents, carers and families are by far the most important influence on children's lives. Those family members who take on a supportive role in their children's learning make a huge difference in terms of health, achievement and behaviour. Sir Christopher Ball strongly emphasised this in the Start Right Report (1994):

> Parents are the most important people in their children's lives. It is from parents that children learn most, particularly in the early months and years… The closer the links between parents and nursery…the more effective that learning becomes.[2]

The view from above

The Government has made it clear that all services that young children and families come into contact with must understand how they can best support child development in its broadest sense. As practitioners we have a responsibility to put the families and parents that we are working with at the centre of our work. The Early Years Framework has a renewed emphasis on the importance of working closely with families in order to support children to reach their full potential. New stronger partnerships between health and early years services should lead to better integrated working. Professor Sir Michael Marmot's review of health inequalities indicates the priority now placed on the early years. He maintains that providing every child with the best start in life is now seen as crucial in reducing health inequalities across the whole life course. He indicates his belief that: '*The foundations for virtually every aspect of human development – physical, intellectual and emotional – are laid in early childhood.*'[3]

Healthy children, healthy lives

This chapter will focus specifically on a number of case studies related to improvements in practice and working partnerships with parents. Each presents opportunities for increasing levels of activity but individually they demonstrate how everyday activities can lead to improved knowledge of healthy eating, higher levels of well-being and involvement and clear opportunities for building strong partnerships with parents. The case studies include a range of different types of settings whose staff understand the need to work towards achieving a greater understanding of health, movement and physical development.

The first case study is an allotment project initiated in a pack away preschool. (A pack away preschool is a preschool without its own building that operates in a community space such as a church hall or community centre and has to pack everything away each day and set up again each morning.) The driving force behind the project was a desire to get children outdoors more often and improve the physical and sensory experiences offered when space is restricted, such as in a church hall. The reported improvements have benefited the children, families and staff in multiple ways, by the gaining of new knowledge and understanding about fresh fruit and vegetables, improving well-being and physical health, and strengthening the relationships between the setting, families and the community. The learning opportunities at the allotment were always more active and physical, with tasks such as digging, planting and watering developing gross motor skills, but additional jobs, such as tying the tomatoes onto the canes, helping develop the children's fine motor skills. Families were engaged in the project from the start and now regularly visit the allotment at the weekend to water, harvest and simply enjoy spending time meeting others. All the fruit, vegetables and flowers grown on the plot are sold to the families, and the children's enthusiasm to try new foods has increased dramatically. Most importantly, as Alan Titchmarsh discusses so powerfully, it sets children up with patterns for life that may last a lifetime:

School was never my favourite place. I was a bit of a late developer academically so my interests tended to fly, wriggle and grow outside the classroom. Luckily for me, I stumbled on the magical world of gardening. From the minute my grandfather took me to his allotment, I was hooked for life. Watching how plants grew and getting my hands dirty brought fun and learning together. It also played to my strengths – determination, single-mindedness and an ability to work with my hands. Looking back, what I learned on my grandfather's plot has set me up for life.[4]

Figure 6.1 *Sets a pattern for life*

The active participation of parents in the life of the school is an essential component of the Reggio Emilia educational experience. Families are actively involved in meetings, conferences, celebrations and events. Parents become a part of the school by not only receiving feedback from teachers about their child's work but also participating when decisions about the school and about educational approaches are taken.

Developing physical outdoor experiences in a pack away preschool – the leader's story

As Tinkerbell Preschool is a pack away setting it comes with its challenges – one of which is the outside area. We are very lucky to have a large outside space; however we are limited to what we can do in the garden; no equipment can be left out and we are not allowed to have any permanent areas for digging, sand play and water play. The children have lots of opportunities for physical activity outdoors but we wanted to give the children the opportunity to be able to dig, explore and grow their own fruit and vegetables so we initially purchased small garden pots and started by growing strawberries and runner beans. The children were able to care for the plants, watch them grow and look after them which they took pride in. However, we received a letter from the hall committee explaining that we had to remove all pots because of health and safety requirements. This is where our journey began and we have never looked back.

After seeing an advert in the village newsletter for new allotments which are situated a ten-minute walk from the setting, I made the decision to put our name down on the waiting list. Unbelievably we were allocated a very large plot within a few weeks. The children have been actively involved in all aspects of the allotment project; this began with the children and the parents being invited to discuss their ideas, drawing pictures and discussing what they would like to see. The parents also saw the benefits and started to raise funds so we could purchase a shed and some gardening tools and then the hard work began. News that the preschool had a plot travelled fast within the allotment community and other plot holders were very supportive, offering help and providing seedlings of various vegetables and showing the children around their plots. The children, parents and staff worked really hard over the year. The children spent months moving piles of soil, manure and bark chippings, planting strawberries, runner beans, cabbages, potatoes and onions. A mini-beast hotel was built; this was a simple and easy construction project offering the children additional opportunities to be physical and work together. The result provided a wonderful investigation area for the children with a never-ending supply of insects that emerge in differing weather conditions.

Children love the physical aspects of digging, watering and harvesting the vegetables. Our first harvest was extremely good considering it was a new experience for the whole team. All the vegetables were taken back to the setting and sold to the parents to fundraise for next year's seeds and plants. We visit the plot on a regular basis so the children are able to observe, discuss and record subtle changes in the environment, during our walk there and at the allotments. During each visit the children understand that they have jobs to do such as planting and weeding; however, there is always time to explore in their own way, whether they play in the house, dig, make mud pies or sit on the log seats sharing a story. The finished plot includes a mini-beast hotel, raised beds for planting, a wooden potting shed come playhouse, a sandpit and large tractor tyres filled with mud, which the children use for digging and planting, and a seating area of logs. Our journey began because we wanted the children to be able to grow their own fruit and vegetables. Together the children, parents and staff have created a wonderful natural area which provides the children with physical activity, space, a new community and an extraordinary resource where each and every area of the Foundation Stage can be explored.

Seeing the journey from an idea to reality – the observer's story

I first heard about the idea for Tinkerbells to take on a plot in the community allotments in Iwade in Kent from the leader in the spring of 2011. The idea took shape from discussions on the limited provision of outdoor experiences for the children as the setting was not permitted to plant and grow anything in the large village-hall garden.

The proactive leader and owner of the preschool applied and was allocated an allotment. Parents and children were invited to bring their ideas to the project through consultation and questionnaires. Children were encouraged to participate and discuss with their parents by writing down or drawing pictures what they would like to have, see or do on visits to the allotment. This provided the basis for planning and the child's voice was evident as they were listened to by practitioners. For example, one child wanted a dragon and this was realised with a statue in the allotment. Funding was raised with parents' help to purchase a shed with toilet facilities, gardening tools and materials to create flower, vegetable and fruit beds and a large sand pit. Staff and parent volunteers gave their time and resources willingly to create an exciting natural space to be enjoyed by children and staff.

Observing the beginnings

I was privileged to accompany a group of eight children and three practitioners to the new allotment in November 2012. The ten-minute walk from the preschool hall through the village and housing estate provided the children and staff with much material for conversation about features in the environment, traffic, buildings, weather and planting in gardens. Staff and children seemed relaxed, staff giving children time to walk at their own pace and giving prompts for conversations. On arrival the children were able to access tools to dig the plot, and staff and children planted daffodils for the following spring. Children showed high levels of well-being and their motivation and involvement were high. Some children just enjoyed the space and freedom to move about, filling buckets and the wheel barrow with soil and transporting it to different areas of the bare land and tipping it out. There were opportunities for children to see other allotment owners working their land and have a chat. A sense of belonging to a community was high. However, not all staff were enthusiastic to take their turn to visit the allotment, preferring to stay indoors, especially in adverse weather.

Observing the outcomes

I was invited again to see the development of the allotment in May 2012 and developments were evident. On a visit with a group of eight children and two practitioners I saw a well-developed space with vegetable, fruit and flower areas, and planted tubs; all guarded by the dragon as requested by one of the children. A toilet had been installed with a privacy curtain, water barrel and composter. A wooden play house and large, covered sand pit had been added, and big tyres and wooden tree stumps provided opportunities for sitting, admiring the space and talking to peers and staff. Children and staff were having their mid-morning snack, sitting together talking about the strawberries which needed watering. Staff and children spent time watering plants, weeding and enjoying the outdoors. A bug hotel in a gravelled area gave another area to explore. What was clear to me, observing the children and staff, was the enjoyment gained from this area without any toys being provided; only working tools for the garden and the children developing exciting role play and cooperating with each other. Staff I spoke to, who were previously reluctant to take their turn to go to the allotment, were now keen to accompany the children as they acknowledged what could be gained from the experience. There is a sense of belonging to this allotment community and the added benefit of the preschool is clearly visible. I even saw a parent with a young child on a neighbouring plot approaching the leader for information about the preschool and asking about a place for her child.

Thus an idea and a vision had become reality with the commitment of continuous reflection on how to make the space even more appealing and workable for children and staff. This space provides the children with regular opportunities for physical development as well as an environmental experience. If we want children to look after the environment we need to nurture a love for it, and give them hands–on, active involvement. Tinkerbells is achieving this for their children.

Manor House Forest School working in partnership with the community

The second case study involves a number of children's centres in an area identified as one of the most deprived local authority district areas in the South East. More importantly, the project worked with families in a ward acknowledged as the most deprived, placing it in the top two per cent in England. For these children the benefits of such interventions in terms of health and education can be life changing. Only half (some 44 per cent) of children living in the most deprived areas achieve a good level of development at five compared to almost 70 per cent of those living in the least deprived areas. Therefore the focus of the project was on improving engagement, raising communication levels and stregthening relationships. The proposed outcomes included developing trust, confidence and self-esteem in addition to supporting all aspects of communication. In addition the sessions would demonstrate the importance of physically active play in natural spaces which included the park, woods and beach, with an emphasis on these areas being within walking distance and free to use. The sessions were planned monthly on Saturday mornings and the families were consulted regularly to guide activities, group sizes and changing environments. Feedback from families provided invaluable insight into changes in the children's behaviour, communication and engagement.

Dads matter: increasing confidence, communication and trust

Working in partnership with the local children's centres has been a rewarding journey both in terms of sharing practice and improving our presence within the community. Before the project started groups of staff from a number of centres came out to experience first-hand the opportunities available in their local area at Forest School. They visited in a particularly wet spring when regular downpours left the woodland area both greener and muddier than usual. This however did not deter the activity levels, with groups of staff enthusiastically working together to build shelters and collect any remaining dry firewood to start a fire. Several of the staff that day were local parents who had started as volunteers at the centres or had been on the parent committee. Having grown up in the local area they thought about their own childhood and the freedom and space that they took for granted. By the end of the day everyone was covered in mud, but exhilarated, leaving with a new understanding of the benefits of challenging active play in natural spaces both in terms of physical development but additionally for building resilience, relationships, trust and communication. The importance of working with the family is seen by Barnardo's as key to promoting resilience (the ability to deal with adversity and stress in life and bounce back), improving educational experiences, and giving children a greater sense of agency and voice.[5]

To engage more interest, a display board with photographs from the staff taster sessions was introduced in two children's centres, and parents started to show an interest. It was decided that twelve Saturday morning sessions would be booked with a focus on engaging primarily with dads and granddads as a target group. Importantly, as the Forest School had four male and two female practitioners it was seen as offering positive male role models both for the children and in terms of the relationships that needed to be built with the fathers, many of whom felt alienated from the world of education and viewed the centre with suspicion.

Many parents, and indeed some practitioners, would question the benefits of children playing out in the cold and rain, therefore it was important to engage parents from the start of the project, to see the huge potential offered by the changes in weather. Waterproof clothing was purchased by the centres and parents were encouraged to supply suitable footwear. Usually by the end of a twelve-week period the group had enjoyed all that the English weather had to offer and rain was often welcomed and enjoyed the most!

Generally, feedback from practitioners at the start of any new programme suggests a general lack of engagement between the adults and children, with little cooperative play and limited communication – usually limited to instruction rather than interest or support. The children initially either stay very close to their familiar adult or push the boundary rules, requiring constant visual monitoring. (Forest School rules require children to be within sight of an adult or within a pre-discussed and visual boundary, often a blue rope.) Gradually, as the sessions build and trusting relationships are established, it can be seen that the well-being and involvement levels of both the adults and children improve dramatically. The fathers communicate more openly and seem to share a new understanding with their children. The visual signs observed in the later sessions are compatible with the indicators of high levels of well-being defined by Leuven and include outward signs of happy, relaxed children with plenty of smiles.[6] Their play is spontaneous, animated and full of energy, and observations include children humming or singing during activities, often lost in their own thoughts. These indicators suggest that the children are becoming open to the outdoor environment demonstrating increased self-confidence and self-assurance. As levels of involvement improve, the children are seen to become more and more engrossed and active in their play. They demonstrate continuous and intense activity with higher levels of concentration, persistence, creativity and energy – all extremely important indicators for future success both at school and in later life. At the end of one session a five-year-old boy, whose father found him hard to manage, spontaneously lay down in the woods and when asked what he was doing replied *'this is the best life I ever had'*. It is changes such as these that drive our work with these families forward and remind us of the things that matter to children: the relationships children have with their families is far more important than the structure of the family. Alongside this, the freedom, autonomy and choice offered at Forest School gives children opportunities often lacking in today's world.[7]

A three-form-entry infant school

The final case study relates to a large local infant school with a reception intake of ninety children per year group. I felt it important to include this example as the school Head demonstrated leadership, vision and insight. I so often hear staff who work in schools dismiss active play as if it has no place in a school. A student recently described outdoor play in her reception class as a very structured process for six children at a time to undertake a planned activity. With children starting in reception at such a young age it is essential that they have environments both indoor and outdoor that facilitate movement as a bedrock of all other development.

Creating a space for play and movement

The Foundation unit is large and airy and each classroom has access to an enclosed outdoor area that is safety surfaced. A large shed is positioned nearby to enable the classroom assistants easy access to the resources. The school is very popular in the area and always oversubscribed. At their last Ofsted inspection in July 2011 the reception unit, made up of three classes of thirty children, was graded as outstanding. In September 2011 a new Head took over the school following the retirement of the previous Head. Her concerns after settling into the position were outlined to the school governors and included, as a priority, the development of a much larger, much more natural outdoor space for the reception children. She wanted the youngest children to have a much more exciting outdoor space, with slopes, gulleys, fountains, vegetable plots and wildlife areas instead of the kit, fence and carpet that has become the norm in many schools and centres.

Her decision and persistence in driving the project forward have been both brave and challenging, particularly as the unit had recently been graded as outstanding, which she was constantly being reminded of. Luckily the school had money in its budget and the governors were persuaded by her argument for more exciting active play for its health and educational benefits. During the spring term new plans were drawn up with parents and children involved at every stage. A number of site meetings were arranged with parents, including those whose children were due to start the following September. Initial ideas were discussed, developed and altered with new ideas submitting and specialist help offered. One mother works with ceramics and glass and has been commissioned to create a plaque and a covered walkway. The new area was opened in September 2012 and the staff and children are currently reviewing it. It will incorporate areas to investigate nature and life cycles, light, shadow and reflection, water and movement, weather and seasons and to encourage physical, gross motor development.

What the outdoor area will include

A much larger natural area will be created without a separate fence or safety surface, with hardwearing sports grass, mud and sand surrounded by a boundary of trees, bamboo and flowering shrubs. A paved roadway will be created for children to use peddle bikes or cars. Rather than the large permanent structure in the centre of the area to climb on, there will be banks, slopes, tyres, planks and a climbing wall adjacent to the large sand pit. Den-building kits will be available with materials for children to create lookouts and hideaways to encourage creativity, imagination and problem solving. A large square area will be sectioned off to create an allotment type gardening area with raised beds, a scarecrow, outdoor tap and composter. A water butt will be included to gather the water from the roof. A covered area running between two of the classrooms will be created incorporating coloured light in the roof panels, mirrors and a mosaic plaque. Coloured pots of herbs will line the path and bamboo wind chimes will be hung. Large cream sails will provide shade and some shelter from the rain. A water pump with shallow gulleys and drains will run along the back wall (this has been one of the most contentious issues because of the fear of children constantly getting wet). An assortment of large loose parts (scrap items) will be kept in the shed for the children to access independently and use in their own way, promoting creativity, critical thinking, imagination and cooperative play.

Challenges and dilemmas

It is important to consider carefully how each early years setting, regardless of its size or location, works to support the engagement and interest of families.

- Parents and children both have rights.
- Being a parent is a complex and difficult role.

- Parents' support plays a vital role at all stages of education; that role needs to be explicit.
- Parenting is a key concern to both men and women.
- How do you create a culture of high expectation?
- Consider how you support and engage parents?
- Do parents feel included and consulted?
- How are children's interests and development shared with parents?
- We must always remember what parents do with their children matters more than who they are.

CHAPTER 7

The different worlds of boys and girls

> I believe our approach to gender relationships in early years settings over the past twenty years has served to harden rather than challenge stereotypical behaviour. This approach is characterised by the corrective and sometimes punitive form of response offered to active young boys in counterpoint to the celebratory response given to compliant and passive young girls playing in the home corner or at the writing table. Both these responses should give us cause for concern.[1]

This chapter begins with an observation of play seen this summer on a local beach. It was at the end of the day with a mixed group of young children ranging from two to approximately seven years old. As it was nearing six o'clock, the beach and surrounding promenade were emptying and the children had more space to play. As I watched, they tipped the contents of several buckets onto the promenade in front of a beach hut. Their miscellaneous treasures, collected that day, included shells, pebbles, driftwood, seaweed, a crab's claw and chalk. While the girls generally used more language to discuss and describe where each item was found, the boys carefully examined, categorised and confirmed the value and future potential of each. The crab's claw was thought particularly worthy and much negotiation was evident as to its ownership! One of the older girls took a piece of chalk and began to draw on the promenade in front of her parents' beach hut. The rest of the group watched or joined in either drawing or attempting to write. This was seen as valuable and actively encouraged by the adults nearby.

The two-year-old, however, began to bang his chalk on the paving, relishing the resulting splintering and dust created. Eagerly he mixed the chalk dust with the sand using his fingers and his enjoyment was obvious. He was engrossed in his new-found game, squealing with delight that each movement produced a reaction not seen before. As the chalk deteriorated into smaller and smaller pieces, he decided to try both hands, now alternating between banging each piece together and marking the paving. Usually, learning would be led by older, more knowledgeable children but on this day it was the inquisitiveness and creativity of the youngest child that altered the interest and play of the group. The older children began to copy his actions, banging their chalk onto the promenade, creating a pattern of marks that covered an increasing area. All the children were completely engrossed; some adding water to the mix to create a paste-like substance that they began to rub onto their bodies. I was reminded of the ritualistic body painting of tribes in wider cultures. Within minutes, however, this small group of children exploring the properties of chalk raised such alarm in nearby adults that the play was stopped. It was deemed to be inappropriate and destructive. In fact it was a worth-while activity initiated by a two-year-old boy trying to make sense of his world by learning, as any good researcher would, through trial and error. The resulting marks were as valuable as the drawing and writing close by; however, the adults' lack of understanding resulted in the play being curtailed and the children frustrated.

The above scenario unfortunately highlights the lack of understanding and narrow-mindedness now often seen in our society. These restrictions on play that were once common place in childhood are having a negative influence on children's development. As a society we seem to have lost sight of the need for such experiences, which are especially necessary for young boys. Tim Gill describes an example of a group of boys building a camp in the woods who were arrested and cautioned. Unbelievably, the police referred to the case as low-level crime.[2] This situation is confusing for children, who are shaped by the messages they receive from the important adults around them. Boys' play may at times be noisier and more physical and they may often find it more difficult to sit still and concentrate for extended periods of time. This can be challenging for practitioners but surely it is their responsibility as educators to ensure that the activities and opportu-nities that are provided meet the needs of all children and not just to reward and encourage those who are generally compliant by nature. As a mother of five boys, and as a practitioner, I want to challenge the assumptions related to boys' behaviour and highlight their genuine need to move and be physical.

The gender debate

The way we behave, think and feel as humans is undoubtedly formed by the socialisation processes that begin shortly after birth. That moment defines how each of us is shaped to fit into the gendered expectations of the prevailing society and culture that we find ourselves in. The stereotypical image of a female child in the Western culture is often gentle, quiet, well-behaved and sensitive. Alternatively, boys are seen as being more physical, robust and troublesome. On occasion it may seem that some adults have such fixed assumptions about boys' behaviour that they miss the important qualities that they bring to their lives. Those inquisitive little boys, mixing their mud and water and trialling how much wet sand sticks when you throw it at the wall, may well go on to become the much needed scientists of the future. As a nation we need the risk takers and creative minds who will think outside the box in order to find new solutions to everyday problems. Our assumptions about girls should equally be challenged. Greater numbers of girls drop out of all physical activity at school at an earlier and earlier age. Establishing physical activity as essential to health and happiness early in life may not be seen yet as 'preparing children for school', but will undoubtedly lead to improvements in mental health, with raised levels of self-esteem, independence and self-resilience. Therefore we need to consider what we expect of boys and girls. Do our expectations somehow shape the experiences for these children?

Figure 7.1 *Our assumptions about girls need to be challenged*

The messages and common assumptions relating to gender seem to be far more evident today than in previous generations. Cordelia Fine, author of *Delusions of Gender*, discusses in depth the relatively recent dress code that now exists, even for new-borns.[3] It was not uncommon in the nineteenth century for young children to be routinely dressed in similar types of cotton smocks for at least the first five years. However, now the media, advertising and fashion trends seem to be cashing in and reinforcing the existing divides. Walk around the clothing department of any high-street store and look at the images and slogans found on young children's clothing. Items on sale for children from babies upwards include, for girls, pastel colours, incorporating butterflies, flowers, hearts, smiling faces and slogans such as 'daddy's little princess' or 'sweet as a button'. Recent conversations with parents in the nursery setting have centred on a particular brand of very expensive footwear designed and marketed for little girls. They perfectly fit into the 'princess' model with added glitter and sparkle and each pair comes with a lipstick and hair slide.

For boys of the same age a different agenda seems to have been predetermined; darker colours suggest the need to cope with more mess, with images that include sport, animals, vehicles or superhero characters. Slogans equally emphasise difference, suggesting 'boys will be boys', and that they are universally tougher, more mischievous and often lazier. These differences in attitudes and expectations that our society places on children can have real consequences and can make it difficult for practitioners to be objective, especially if their own personal experiences of being around boys is limited. When we divide the world into two very specific groups, male and female, this way we are inclined to see each group with completely different traits. In reality, boys and girls are different; they may exhibit different interests, activity levels, emotional reactions, physical strengths and attention spans. But equally it must be accepted that same-sex children also differ. No two children are the same, therefore we must get to know each child and provide opportunities based on the evidence about each child rather than use generalisations. Leading a Forest School nursery setting, I have found that each year sees an increase in the demand for places for boys, with parents now recognising the more physical outdoor experiences as a necessity for them. However, I would argue that these experiences are just as essential for girls, who relish opportunities to break away from what can sometimes be suffocating, overprotective parenting or an overemphasis on quiet, indoor activities.

The repeated message that appears to resonate both here in the UK and more recently in the US, Australia and Canada suggests that, generally, boys' development continues to lag behind that of girls', not just throughout the early years but throughout their entire schooling. In addition boys are four times more likely to be excluded from school than their female classmates. Boys are known to be at greater risk of speech delay or of developing one of the major learning and development disorders. Statistics suggest that at least four times as many boys are diagnosed with autism, hyperkinetic disorders (attention deficit disorder) or dyslexia than girls. Steve Biddulph, author of *The Secret of Happy Children, Raising Boys*, and *The New Manhood* voices his concerns and questions many of the existing assumptions relating to boys' development. '*A better world depends on making all groups happier and healthier. If we want more good men in the world, we must start treating boys with less blame and more understanding.*'[4]

It is known that, in general, boys develop more slowly in the areas of language, self-control and fine motor skills, but are often accomplished at spatial and mechanical tasks. As downward pressure is applied in settings and homes and academic expectations are increased, this early start is becoming much more of a substantial handicap. This is particularly evident when boys progress from the more active play-based reception class to a more structured classroom in year one, often with limited opportunities for movement.

> We regularly see boys in KS1 who are unwilling (or unable) to take instructions, who are impulsive, struggle to reflect on their behaviour (when they have done something wrong), are easily wound up by others, distracted, over-physical and are seemingly unable to show self-control.
>
> *Year one teacher*[5]

Engaging these boys in far more practical, hands-on physical experiences would be more effective. I know this from previous experience with my son who was just five when he entered year one. He was an eager little boy, interested in everything but he found the school experience not just difficult but a place that he perceived was not for him. Just one year earlier at four he had started with such enthusiasm and excitement following in the footsteps of his three elder siblings. Being a kinaesthetic learner he needed activities that would engage his intellect alongside his hands, rather than the constant handwriting practice, which he describes as a twenty-year-old 'as physical torture'. It was later discovered that he had not only underdeveloped fine muscles in his hands, but the constant dribbling that resulted in saturated clothing was a result of underdeveloped muscles in his lips and mouth. These signs are important for practitioners to be aware of both in terms of developing the skills for handwriting but also for speech.

An article in the *Times Educational Supplement* back in 2008 described how one primary school had focused particularly on the important transition to year one by getting each pupil to visit a nearby woodland one morning a week, come rain or shine. The activities on offer included an emphasis on physical development and risk taking in an attempt to counter the pervading 'cotton wool culture'. The Head recently commented that, *'the best classrooms look as if learning just happens'*.[6] It is important to consider carefully the needs of the children and the experiences on offer in all classrooms for young children. Many boys may prefer to work on the floor, and write lying on their backs with paper taped under tables. They may prefer to problem solve with large construction blocks rather than using worksheets sitting at tables. Three-seater trikes offer opportunities for fine and gross motor skills alongside communication, teamwork and negotiation of social rules. Offering experiences that combine physical alongside cognitive development, such as a woodwork bench with real tools and wood or recycled resources such as the inspirational Bristol Scrap-pod project, helps bring learning alive.

PlayPods case study, Bristol, October 2011

By introducing an assortment of large and small scrap pieces (the term is 'loose parts'), rather than conventional play resources in school playgrounds, children have been enabled to be really creative in their play; the items are non-prescriptive and inspire a range of different play types. The physical and human environment within schools is improved, creating stimulating and interactive spaces where children can learn through play. Feedback from the acting Head of one primary school indicates:

> The children are playing more collaboratively and the variety of things they get up to is huge. They're really inventive and they're learning new skills all the time. When they're building things and looking at how pieces fit together they're dealing first hand with the laws of physics. And of course there's a great physical side to it too – using muscles and burning up energy. The staff are really excited about having the PlayPod too and have embraced it in a really positive way. Everyone agrees that it's hugely improved play times and greatly improved

the adults' attitude and knowledge of play. They're risk assessing play but allowing the children to take more risks of their own. The number of bumps and bruises might have gone up but children are learning their own boundaries which will help keep them safer in the future.

I would wholeheartedly recommend the PlayPod ... every school should have one.[7]

Rethinking classroom experiences to include ones that encourage children to be more physical and actively involved encompasses both the mind and the body; or, as Cambridge mathematician Jacob Bronowski states:

the hand is the cutting edge of the mind... In the end, the march of man is the refinement of the hand in action. The most powerful drive in the ascent of man is his pleasure in his own skill. He loves to do what he does well and, having done it well, he loves to do it better.[8]

In addition, Bill Lucas and Guy Claxton argue in their book *New Kinds of Smart* that teachers and educationists must rethink their understanding of intelligence.[9] The book identifies real-life intelligence as '*imagination, perseverance, perceptiveness and collaboration*' and highlights '*self-discipline and resilience*' developed in the Foundation years as counting for much more in predicting school success than the notion of IQ.

The need to consider brain development

One of the most important considerations when thinking about brain development is to acknowledge its plasticity; that is, to accept that experiences change brains. Our brains are extremely malleable in childhood, more than at any other stage of life, and can be modified and changed in response to experience and stimuli. It is important to remember that every physical or sensory experience is passed through the nervous system triggering new cells, neurons and synapses that respond, adapt and expand capabilities. Therefore the early experiences that practitioners plan for are, quite simply, creating the brains of the future. So it is critical to get this planning right for children who are spending ten or more hours each day in a setting. Scientists now seem to agree that brain development is an intricate weave of nature and nurture. The environments young children and babies find themselves in shapes the unique gene pool of each child. For example a child's height or weight is often predetermined by their genes but both are highly dependent on the nutrition and eating habits established in childhood.

Another important consideration here is the argument that gender behaviour and identity are hard wired from an early age and that differences between male and female brains are influenced by their exposure to different genes and hormones. Testosterone begins to surge in a boy's brain only six weeks after conception; however by birth there is little difference in the levels of either sex. Studies on animals seem to suggest that this early exposure to testosterone at the start of life, in vitro, seems to drive the male tendency towards more aggressive or impulsive play. Michael Gurian discusses how practitioners need a genuine understanding of the essential differences in the physical development of girls and boys, so that they can establish strategies to help boys cope with what can be challenging situations.[10]

RAAAH!! – It's all about dinosaurs!

Like many boys aged four, Joseph loves dinosaurs. He currently makes daily requests for information about dinosaurs, much of it from watching small clips from films, animations and documentaries. He has dinosaur toys that he uses to act out battles, comparing their varying physical attributes and requesting regular predictions from those adults he perceives as important, which dinosaur they consider will win. We play role-play games as dinosaurs too, acting out 'fights' with some rough-and-tumble play.

Joseph is interested in the way the earth looked when the dinosaurs were around and is fascinated by volcanos and extreme weather. When he draws, he often depicts scenes of stormy clouds and flashes of lightening that break the trees, with erupting volcanos and dinosaurs roaming. A couple of days ago Joseph requested a film called *Night at the Museum* which includes scenes of visitors looking at dinosaur bones. Afterwards we decided to make our own dinosaur bones. We collected sticks at the park and the boys all had fun painting them white. I had planned that we might make a dinosaur skeleton picture by sticking them to black paper, but Joseph had other ideas and was determined to make something three-dimensional. We constructed a head, neck and body by tying the sticks together with string. This was as much as Joseph wanted to do; he didn't feel a need to give his model any legs so we didn't! He said it was a duckbill dinosaur and that it's head was a crest. He put his dinosaur on a pile of blue wool that he said was the water. Joseph is a fan of Julia Donaldson's book *Tyrannosaurus Drip*[11] and it seems that he was inspired by the duckbill dinosaurs in this. Joseph said he'd like to make a land for his dinosaur to live in, inside a box with volcanos! I'm sure this will be our next project. After the dinosaur was made he wanted me to film him playing with it, and then filmed me talking about it. When we made puppets recently at a workshop at our local gallery he asked to film his results in action there too. The huge asteroid that hit earth during the time dinosaurs roamed the earth fascinates Joseph, and one weekend sees an impressive meteor shower in our skies that he has been talking excitedly about. He asked us to set an alarm for the middle of the night so that he can watch them!

In just a few days, Joseph's fascination with dinosaurs has touched on elements of history, biology, geography, literature and astronomy as well as role play, art and craft and physical activity. What I really love about this is that I feel as though I am simply playing with him, enjoying his company and helping him pursue his ideas. We are simply having fun together, and this is possibly because I know that wherever this play and his ideas flow, he is learning something that is meaningful for him.

Boys' interests in dinosaurs seem to emerge in almost all settings between the ages of three and four and have been successfully extended and planned into Forest School sessions in the woods. One such dinosaur dig led to the children excavating an area of the woods to find large 'glow in the dark' bones that had been buried the day before. The practitioners had planned the session around two particular boys who were equally interested in dinosaurs; one rarely came out to the woods, the other had been involved in several biting incidents both at home and in the setting. These incidents had been linked to him role playing being a dinosaur. This session was planned to offer opportunities to raise self-confidence, improve physical dexterity using tools and encourage the quieter boy to join the outdoor session. The children dug with enthusiasm and excitement, sharing finds with each other; many other objects were discussed and evaluated before the first bone was unearthed. A discussion of the size and shape of the dinosaur followed with the children demonstrating their in-depth knowledge and enthusiasm. Was it a meat eater? How would they know? Would they find a triceratops? During this time one male leader talked quietly alongside the boy who had been involved in the biting incidents. They discussed how sharp dinosaur teeth were and how they would have been bigger than his teeth. They then each bit into an apple and discussed how sharp human teeth were. Once all the bones were unearthed the group carried the bones to a grassy area where they shared a drink and exchanged conversations, reflecting on their finds. Then followed a prediction of how big the dinosaur was as they set about working together to figure out what a complete dinosaur skeleton looked like. The practitioners had brought tape-measures, rulers, paper and notepads to record alongside cameras and the children's video cameras. It is often found that boys in particular are drawn to the ICT equipment. On returning to the setting the children engaged in further research using the preschool library and the computers to find different images, which were printed off to take home. Following the interests of the children in this way opens up opportunities to discuss difficult feelings, encourages motivation and socialisation, extends conversations and helps strengthen parental partnerships.

The role of positive male role models

There can be no denying that the early years workforce is imbalanced, with males only accounting for somewhere between two and four per cent of the early years workforce. This imbalance must be addressed in order to make the early years teams more representational within the community and to broaden the experiences for all children and families. Both Claire Tickell's report looking at the EYFS[12] and Cathy Nutbrown's review of early years qualifications specify the need to recruit more male early years professionals in England.[13] While it is important not to stereotype male practitioners as simply being there to provide more physical rough-and-tumble outdoor play, it is important to acknowledge the qualities that a more balanced workforce brings. Male practitioners are more likely to share, or at least relate to, the same interests of the boys than some female staff. In addition my own experience (currently employing five male practitioners) suggests that they seem more able to motivate and inspire them. '*By watching a person we admire in action, our brain takes in a cluster of skills, attitudes and values.*'[14] A strong male role model who actively joins in and supports superhero play will be, at times, cavorting and play fighting but equally will also be designing and constructing weapons, tools, hideouts or capes. This support not only enhances the child's creativity but enables them to begin to learn life-long skills related to self-control, playing by the rules and showing respect. This type of play has been observed in young males across different cultures and is often linked back to the hunter–gatherer societies where boys needed to practise speed, energy and strength. However, this is regularly the type of play discouraged by predominantly female staff who lack the understanding and simply see it as fighting or aggression, immediately closing it down. Early years researcher Penny Holland argues that when young children play fight or engage in superhero play they are learning invaluable lessons related to social skills. According to psychologists, such experiences enable children to convey feelings using facial expressions and body language and further understand their peer group and position in it. Nevertheless, she reminds us that '*children's play behaviour is not carved in stone and is amenable to sensitive practitioners, like sculptors, working with, rather than against the grain of children's play.*'[15] The final message here is clear; all children learn more when they are respected for who they are, and early years practitioners engage in the learning process with them on a physical and emotional level, regardless of their gender. It is all too easy to stereotype children even if the process is unconscious. Society differentiates between boys and girls from birth in a number of ways: from their dress code to how we relate to them and more especially how we expect them to behave. Children very rapidly pick up from adults how it is appropriate for a boy or girl to behave and will often seek to fit into these roles. Boys are no less able than girls, so we need to ask ourselves what we can do in order to better understand why they appear to be making less progress in the EYFS and beyond. The quality of meaningful relationships with them and the beliefs we hold will leave a lasting impression on their ability to engage confidently in the learning process.[16]

Challenges and dilemmas

- How do you recognise and challenge assumptions related to gender?
- How do you find out what inspires and motivates the boys in your setting?
- Do you regularly check that images in the setting challenge stereotypes?
- What steps do you take to ensure all children take part in activities, regardless of gender?
- Consider how you can help staff see boys in a more positive light. In what ways do you support rough-and-tumble play?
- Are allowances made for differences in physical maturity?
- What do you know about impulse control and how can you support boys to develop it?

- Do you need to encourage girls to be more physical and boys more caring?
- Be aware of your own responses to boys when their play involves weapons.
- How can your setting encourage more positive male role models to be part of young children's lives?

CHAPTER 8

Forest School

The roots of life and learning

> If the child has enough euphoric outdoor experiences in childhood – experiences in which she feels merged, continuous, at one with the hedge she's hidden in, the baby bird in her hands, the darkened pond – then her affinity for the natural world will never go away. And that affinity will become the soil in which an environmental ethic takes root.[1]

Picture a scene on a chilly December morning when winter mists hang low over the horizon, embracing the trees in the distant parkland. The grass glittering with the morning frost and the colours of the gathered leaves beneath our feet seem richer against nature's new palate. As the children explore, their attention is drawn to a frozen puddle; its contents now incarcerated in the ice. This impromptu stop provides new opportunities for discussions, debates and problem solving. How to dig out the acorn trapped within the ice and '*Would it still be alive?*' '*Would it still be able to grow into a tree?*' One child is puzzled. Another child climbs confidently onto some overturned logs to survey the group from a height. As he climbs he seems aware of the need to take extra care, demonstrating past knowledge of the effects a thin layer of ice can have on his favourite climbing logs. In this ever-changing natural terrain he adjusts his balance using his whole body and negotiates slowly, carefully considering where to place his next step. As another child approaches he enters into a conversation about not slipping, evidence that he understands staying safe; and demonstrating both his understanding, confidence and communication skills.

These regular experiences built up over weeks using the same environment provide these children not only with rich learning opportunities to stretch and extend their capabilities, but interest, motivation and challenge to want to move their bodies and be active. As Tim Gill eloquently describes:

> Natural places are singularly engaging, stimulating, life-enhancing environments where children can reach new depths of understanding about themselves, their abilities and their relationship with the world around them.[2]

The role of Forest Schools in children's physical development has unquestionable long-term positive health implications. The *Lancet Medical Journal* recently published data that suggested: '*the UK has one of the world's least physically active populations*'. The report continued with the warning that the consequences of this inactivity would be responsible for '*as many deaths worldwide as smoking and obesity*'.[3] The paper claims that exercise '*has been called a miracle drug that can benefit every part of the body and substantially extend lifespan*'.[4] Additionally, the outdoor environment itself can be a useful formative evaluation tool for practitioners in understanding and assessing a child's skills and abilities, and in recognising physical changes over time. In a study 'Childhood and Nature' commissioned by Natural England in 2009, evidence suggested '*children spend less time playing in natural places, such as woodlands, countryside and heaths than they did in previous generations. Less than 10% play in such places compared to 40% of adults when they were young*'. Interestingly, 81 per cent of children said that they would like more freedom to play outside.[5] In addition to concerns relating to physical health, evidence seems to indicate that as a nation we appear to be following in the footsteps of America with a second generation of children suffering from 'nature deficit disorder'. This term was coined by Richard Louv to describe the damage he believed was caused to children who never experienced the natural world. It's crucial, he argues, not to shield them from adventures in the great outdoors and the connections these bring to the natural world. In his bestselling book, *Last Child in the Woods*, Richard Louv convincingly debates this concept:

> Nature Deficit Disorder describes the human costs of alienation from nature, among them: diminished use of the senses, attention difficulties, and higher rates of physical and emotional illnesses... Just as children need good nutrition and adequate sleep, they may very well need contact with nature.[6]

Many practitioners cite health and safety concerns limiting the opportunities available; however in the twenty-first century it seems more young children are admitted to British hospitals for injuries sustained falling out of bed than out of trees. '*Broken bones*,' Louv reminds us, '*used to be a rite of passage for children. Now all paediatricians see are cases of obesity and repetitive strain injury.*' While 'nature deficit disorder' is not an accepted medical condition, it has been linked to increased rates of ADHD and mental health difficulties in children. It is thought that children are missing out on the pure delight that comes from daily experiences in the natural world; and, as a result, grow into adults that lack an understanding of the importance of nature to human society. Other substantial evidence suggests that as human beings we have an inborn need for connections with nature: a notion known as 'biophilia'. Initially defined by the psychologist Erich Fromm, it was later popularised by biologist Edward Wilson,[7] who discussed humans' primal urge to connect with nature.

So what can practitioners working in early years education do to combat the joint concerns related to inactivity and nature deficit disorder, in order for young children to fully develop, test their bodies physically, build stamina and discover the natural world for themselves? Many settings may suggest they are not equipped or have no access to natural outdoor spaces, but I have always found that when the motivation is there, settings think in more creative ways, opening up new opportunities for the children and families they support. Importantly there is now a great deal of agreement on this issue both politically and socially with politicians, parents, teachers, doctors, social workers, journalists and the children themselves supporting change. All seem *'united in their belief that children would benefit from greater freedom to explore outdoors'*.[8] A clear message from the latest Good Childhood Report suggests children are happier when given freedom, autonomy and choice, all aspects closely linked to both the EYFS and the Forest School principles. *'Children need agency, and real experiences to connect them to their local community; this responsibility and trust leads to a more contented, meaningful life'*.[9] Consider here Piaget's basic theory in relation to learning; as human beings we are all continually adapting to our environment. But importantly, he maintained that knowledge could not simply be transmitted from one person to another' it must be constructed or invented through our own action.[10]

Unpicking Forest School

The past fifteen years has seen early years settings being bombarded with new initiatives and research all intended to raise standards. In addition to raising quality, the evidence from neuroscience suggests that regular sensory experiences in carefully considered environments are of upmost importance. As a pedagogical approach Forest School is still in the early stages of development in the UK. O'Brien and Murray in a significant research project carried out by the New Economics Foundation and Forest Research defined the approach as:

> An inspirational process that offers children, young people and adults regular opportunities to achieve, and develop confidence and self-esteem through hands-on learning experiences in a woodland environment.[11]

The growing interest in Forest Schools started in Britain in the mid-1990s; they are based on the Scandinavian belief that children, particularly under the age of seven, need regular contact with the outdoors. Students from Bridgwater College in Somerset visited Denmark in 1995 to observe the practice there[12] and returned with enthusiasm about the need for such experiences for young children in England. Since then the number of Forest Schools has grown with trained practitioners leading outdoor sessions in local parks or woodland. The Forest School initiative is gradually spreading to the south of England, with half of all London boroughs now undertaking some kind of Forest School project. New groups and clusters are now forming to enable more experienced practitioners to discuss and reflect on their work, alongside other staff teams, supporting and guiding the development of the concept in England.[13]

Forest School England principles

The Forest School ethos is fundamentally about supporting children to learn at their own pace and for them to follow their own leads and interests as they explore in stimulating environments full of sensory diversity. These regular sessions in local woodland offer a completely different learning experience, one that is constantly changing, providing motivation, stimulation and freedom. Additionally, Forest Schools help settings meet a variety of Government objectives such as 'Healthy Schools', 'Early Intervention' and supporting families to lead healthier and happier lives. Ideally a Forest Schools programme would run over a whole year with the same children so that they fully experience the changing seasons and learn to work together as a group. In addition to the huge benefits this offers in terms of building relationships and communication skills, it allows children to learn about themselves and their physical capabilities, building confidence, core strength, dexterity and stamina, as well as a genuine love of the outdoors.

The Forest School approach has a set of principles which guides its use:

- Forest School is for all children and young people.
- Forest School builds on a child's innate motivation and positive attitude to learning, offering them the opportunities to take risks, make choices and initiate learning for themselves.
- Forest School is organised and run by qualified Forest School leaders.
- Forest School maximises the learning potential of local woodland through frequent and regular experiences throughout the year, not a one-off visit.
- Forest School helps children to understand, appreciate and care for the natural environment.

Setting up a Forest School: a personal story

Setting up and running an outdoor setting, such as a Forest School, is not easy. Initially barriers were faced relating to our first site, particularly as it had public access so attitudes to risk were seen as greater. The weather conditions also proved to be a challenge for some staff and parents as they did not necessarily understand the benefits of taking children out if it was raining or cold. A common comment was, '*All that mess and mud, for what?*' However, equipping staff and children with waterproof clothing from Scandinavia and encouraging parents to join in sessions helped spread the word that the outdoors really did benefit children. Now, three years later, we have the full support of our parents, families and staff team and a second private site enables us to stay as true to the original Forest School ethos as possible. Owing to the use of real tools and the high level of practical tasks, using the woodland as an outdoor 'wild' classroom requires a high ratio of adults to children and strict safety rules and procedures are in force. Daily site assessments are carried out prior to children arriving and all activities are assessed for risk. Staff leading sessions must hold both accredited Forest School training and outdoor paediatric first aid training.

We are all concerned about keeping children safe but professional conversations need to centre on the potential benefits of overcoming hazards or dangers, so that children are encouraged and motivated. By setting clear boundaries but allowing children the freedom to do things they may not normally be able to, Forest Schools promote:

- self-awareness
- self-regulation
- intrinsic motivation
- empathy
- good social communication skills
- independence
- a positive mental attitude, self-esteem and confidence.

Reflections from a Forest School practitioner

When introducing tools in the woods we often start with a potato peeler. These can cut a child's fingers if not used correctly but they are not likely to cause any serious harm. By the time I introduce tools into a Forest School programme I usually know the children well enough to know how they will react, but tools are introduced gradually so we get a feel for how the children respond. From peelers we move on to working with knives and bow-saws. The sensory experience of peeling off bark and creating an object gives children mastery over their environment.

Mastery play is described by Bob Hughes in his taxonomy of play types as '*Control of the physical and affective ingredients of the environments*'.[14] It is often defined as a gross motor activity and can be seen in children building dens, damming streams, laying paths and modifying spaces by clearing or planting. However, there is also the physical, transformative extension of exploratory play. Though it is physical it has an emotional significance too as it allows children to connect with the elements in the environment, developing trust and pride in their achievements. Knowing your children well and discussing the potential risks and benefits with parents beforehand enables each child to take small steps towards mastery.

Sessions at Forest School may involve:

- lighting / managing fires / cooking over fire / stories around the fire
- building dens / imaginative/fantasy play
- climbing trees / rope swings
- using full size tools to cut, carve and create
- creating and representing with natural materials
- playing environmental games.

The importance of risk taking

When I was a child, as with most of my contemporaries, the freedom to play outdoors, often away from any adults, was considered part of a normal childhood. It became the responsibility of the older children in the neighbourhood to keep an eye on the younger ones as they joined their games. Activities were evolved, developed, changed and fought over, but my abiding memories are of fun and excitement. In fact I can still vividly remember climbing out of my bedroom window late at night after a heavy snow fall! The garden was so magical and I felt compelled to be part of it. This type of freedom is now very rare and would be considered by society as 'poor parenting'. So we must ask ourselves how we have travelled so far in fifty years and what the potential consequences may be for today's children. Tanya Byron recently commented on the value of the outdoor area in developing resilient children:

> The less children play outdoors, the less they learn to cope with the risks and challenges they will go on to face as adults... Nothing can replace what children gain from the freedom and independence of thought they have when trying new things out in the open.[15]

In July 2007 the then British government launched a consultation document entitled 'Staying Safe', which opened a debate on the sensible balance needed between protection and freedom. It considered how supporting adults could protect children without wrapping them in cotton wool, impeding independence and robbing them of *'vital opportunities to learn and develop'*.[16]

Figure 8.1 *Explore natural, wild places*

Giving young children the opportunities to explore outdoors throughout the year in natural wild places helps build confidence, self-esteem and communication particularly when working collaboratively, for example den building, collecting wood for the fire or setting the boundary ropes. '*If you watch a child playing outside they're just doing so many physical tasks – they run for hours, dig, climb. If you told them to do it they wouldn't, but they want to because they're playing. You won't get that level of physical activity with anything else.*'[17]

Regular visits to the Forest School also build a deeper appreciation for nature and the cycles of life and death during the changing seasons. On several occasions the children have come across dead animals: a fox, rabbit and fossilised squirrel. Rather than being steered away from such finds the staff engage the children in conversations and give them opportunities to touch, think and reflect on the animals' life and death. Experience suggests that young children are very interested in the details surrounding death but as adults we often avoid the subject with children altogether, believing it would be too upsetting for children to understand. However, rather than being repelled by the dead animal they are highly motivated to explore asking questions relating to its skin, fur, bones, feet, eyes, mouth and teeth. These sensitive explorations are akin to the work of Susan Isaacs at the Malting House School. Here she allowed each child's curiosity to lead the learning in a rich environment including a large garden. Many of the children were sent to her school because of difficulties with emotional development or poor behaviour; I have a similar experience, being in an area identified as one of the most deprived local authority district areas within the South East. However, Isaacs found that the freedom and challenge offered to the children in the outdoor area, with real tools, fires and exciting exploration, resulted in the most wonderful questions and scientific investigations.[18]

Challenging physical play

When children are first introduced to the woods, they often lack confidence and the physical dexterity required in the new environment. It is often outside their current experiences and it can take several sessions for them to begin to really engage in the more physical aspects of the woods. However, as they became more physically confident they begin to find opportunities for climbing and jumping. Children learn to judge the distance that they are happy to climb, negotiating their own safe height. The new perspective offered by the added height motivates most children, increasing their confidence and self-esteem. It has been found that if children are allowed the independence to climb up a tree, they will usually be more than able to climb back down – risk assessing their own capabilities. Forest School practitioners are there to support children's growing independence and will support and encourage a child before lifting them down. The physical aspects of play in the forest environment become increasingly important to the children as the leaders introduce tyres, ropes and tools to extend interest and teamwork.

They often guide the children towards areas of woodland with steep gradients. These 'sliding slopes' as the children refer to them have become one of the most popular parts of the woods we use. The steep gradients offer challenges to the children both in climbing up and either sliding down in the mud or running down avoiding others. They help and support each other to climb. sometimes in convoy, introducing team games with their own rules. Stones, leaves, ropes and sticks are introduced by children as props, batons or markers leading to conversations relating to distance, height and speed. Many of the activities also involve a high level of physical participation using fine motor skills: collecting, whittling, weaving and tying ropes. Above all these activities are often not possible in the confines of an early years setting where conventional climbing equipment is positioned on safety surfacing and strict rules are often applied. In fact on a recent visit to a large setting attached to a children's centre I heard a practitioner tell the children not to run about outside and '*be silly*'. What is this demonstrating about her limited knowledge of child development?

Tree swinging

No Forest School session would be complete without observing a number of children either swinging from a tyre, rope or hanging branch. They seem naturally drawn to these activities, returning to them regularly. Children like the tyre in particular as it allows them to challenge themselves in a number of ways. Consider the physical skills involved as they balance: standing on top of the tyre holding onto the rope above or climbing through the middle layer facing either the forest floor or the tree canopy above. At times several children use one tyre, utilising different areas but negotiating the space, speed and position. These activities not only build physical strength in the arms, shoulders, back, neck and hands which is essential for developing posture, core strength and the grip required for handwriting. But movement of this kind is also vital in supporting the healthy development of the vestibular system within the inner ear. When we tilt our head in any direction, the fluid within the inner ear moves small hairs, indicating our position in space. ('*Are we upside down or upright?*') As the child swings upside down a wealth of information is relayed to the brain in relation to how fast they are moving and which direction they are travelling. It is the vestibular system that coordinates all the sensory information from the eyes, ears, muscles, joints, fingertips and feet and helps regulate our sense of balance. It also helps adjust our blood pressure, heart rate, nervous system and immune responses. In terms of 'school readiness' it is the vestibular system which has the greatest overall effect on our ability to function successfully. Children who have difficulty with body control and balance may have a vestibular system which under-responds to movement. These children often dislike being thrown in the air, floating in water, having their head tipped too far back, swings of any kind or jumping on the trampoline. Any movement that would disrupt the fluid in the inner ear can result in panic or distress. Additionally, because they often have a poor sense of where their body is in terms of personal space, the resulting behaviour can be seen as negative or aggressive especially when others get too close. Some children on the autistic spectrum can present with sensory dysfunction and require sensory stimulation during therapy sessions.

Signs that may suggest poor vestibular function include:

- a delayed loss of primitive reflexes
- delay in gross motor milestones / low muscle tone
- developmental delays, with children clumsy, unable to balance
- a child that easily tires.

We all have an inbuilt need to regulate ourselves through vestibular stimulation, both for calming and arousal. However, our differing levels of need for movement is individual and it is important that practitioners understand that there is no 'normal' requirement. Young babies can be calmed by a gentle rocking movement; similarly, as adults, many of us enjoy the relaxation and calm of a rocking chair. However, not enough movement results in a need to arouse the vestibular system. It is generally accepted that children need more of this stimulation than adults, therefore physical activities that involve spinning, rocking, hanging upside down, or a combination of these, provide each child with the intense movements and sensory experiences that they so often seek.

The Forest School approach is enabling children across the country to access environments that offer complementary experiences to the traditional indoor classroom, or outdoor areas. They provide regular opportunities for active learning in nearby woodland enabling children to build up confidence and competence. The three components of effective learning and teaching identified in the EYFS: active learning, play and exploration, and creativity and critical thinking are obvious to anyone visiting a Forest School session. The children are highly motivated and engaged while 'just playing'; however it is clear that the potential for development is immense.

Challenges and dilemmas

- How can you lead the development of outdoor play in your setting?
- Can you send a practitioner to undertake Forest School training?
- Is there any funding or support from the local authority for this type of venture?
- Is there a local Forest School that you could visit?
- Get to know your local area. What woodland or parkland is within one to five miles of your setting that could offer children an alternative physical environment?
- Do you have trees in your outside area or garden that children can climb or that could support a tyre swing?
- Can natural resources found in the woodland be brought into your setting?
- Think carefully about your understanding of risk: are you limiting children's experiences?

- What hands-on experiences of nature do you provide for children?
- Can you introduce real tools into your setting with activities such as gardening, woodwork or cooking?
- How can you utilise local volunteers or groups to help with a project? Students who are part of the Duke of Edinburgh Award scheme need to do voluntary work and could help. Local Cadet groups, Army, Navy, and Airforce, offer help with clearing grounds and provide excellent role models for young children.

CHAPTER 9

Ready for school or prepared for life?

To be educated is not to have arrived at a destination; it is to travel with a different view. What is required is not feverish preparation for something that lies ahead, but to work with a precision, passion and taste at worthwhile things that lie at hand. These worthwhile things cannot be forced on reluctant minds... They are acquired by contact with those who have already acquired them and who have patience, zeal, and competence enough to initiate others into them.[1]

Imagine the process involved in building a traditional brick built home: plans are drawn up, the land surveyed and eventually building begins with excavation and stabilisation. Different types of land and soil require specialist intervention and support in order to strengthen the footings in order to prevent future difficulties. However, as in all building work this first stage is the most important and vital for the future effectiveness of the home. It is on these foundations that the strength, stability and longevity of the building will rest and although invisible after the house is completed, it is the consideration and attention given at this early stage that will ultimately prevent future problems from arising. The same analogy can be applied when thinking about the most important and influential first stage of life: the Foundation years are just that. It is this foundation that provides the stability, strength and resilience that all humans need to thrive. We are preparing children for so much more than school; we are equipping them with the essential ingredients for a healthy childhood: strong relationships, regular sleep, good food and daily opportunities to be active and physical. The London Olympics was built on the legacy of *inspiring a generation*; we need to capture this and consider how we can both 'inspire' and 'aspire' to reassess our practice to provide better opportunities for children and families within our communities.

It is clear from Government indicators that 'readiness for school' will be a priority for those working in the early years; however it is important for practitioners to deconstruct their understanding of this concept. By focusing simply on the school skills of literacy or numeracy, many children, including a high percentage of boys, may continue to be unfairly branded as failures before the age of seven. Evidence from the Cambridge Review indicates that '*the education of young children matters immeasurably; to them both now and in the future, and to our society'*.[2] Practitioners must set high expectations because no matter what their background or circumstances, young children are born with huge potential. But we must also consider the environments in which young children find themselves. Evidence from teachers in year one classrooms suggest children are already being 'turned off' school, being required to sit still for long periods of the day. Fears are that with the introduction of the phonics test this situation will only get worse. Therefore, as 'schoolification' of young children's lives becomes set more deeply in policy, it is increasingly important for practitioners to be able to question what experiences young children need and deserve in their formative years and what this means in terms of health, learning and well-being.

The definition of education provided at the start of the chapter by Richard Peters reminds us that learning continues throughout life, long before and long after we enter statutory schooling. But learning is not easy and it takes great effort so it is important to think about the learning dispositions we can instil in our children that will not only prepare them for school but provide them with the essential tools for life.

Defending play

While play has been seen to underpin policy in early years practice for many years, there are numerous pressures on practitioners to adopt a more structured school-based approach to learning in order to prepare children for school. I would argue here that, as adults, we don't waste important parts of our life preparing for old age; how often have you practised walking with a Zimmer frame or used a commode just to start getting the hang of it? So why should children practise being five when they are three or four? The vital years before statutory school are precious and need protecting, especially with children starting in reception classes long before the statutory age of five. This is already far sooner than most other countries across the world where the average starting age is much closer to six. Peter Dixon, who cares passionately about the plight of young children in England, writes:

> We must remember young children are not miniature adults, nor are they watered down eight year olds, nine year olds, or thirteen year olds...a five year old is five, he or she is five because she is five and not because she will soon be six or sixty six.[3]

The repeated use of the term 'school readiness' in recent policy documents can be misinterpreted by many including staff, parents and, unfortunately, inspectors, who believe it is related to more direct teaching: sitting down and concentrating on number work or the literacy skills of reading and writing. In fact 'school readiness' is much more related to developing children who see themselves as learners; who are motivated, can communicate well and are independent in thought and action and interact appropriately with others. These key skills of *'motivation, socialisation and self-esteem'* were identified by Sir Christopher Ball in 1994 as part of the Start

Right Report. These were defined as '*the super skills of learning*'.[4] The report emphasised the importance of young children developing a 'can do' attitude, good social skills; being eager to learn, involved, and having a sense of belonging and emotional well-being.

> Our traditional conception of play was that of free, spontaneous, and self-initiated activity that reflected the abundant energy of healthy child development. Today, however, that conception of play has been relegated to the early childhood years. For school aged children, play is now identified with learning and with the preparation for adult life.[5]

The importance of daily physical exercise, movement and play has been discussed extensively throughout the book but in terms of 'school readiness' it must be remembered that '*exercise cues the building blocks of learning in the brain*' and as such is '*the single most powerful tool to optimise brain function*'.[6] So, in order to continually connect and fire synapses in the brain, we need to get children's bodies working hard. In addition we must consider that for many of today's 'backseat children', the physical aspects of life have declined and it therefore becomes even more important within daily practice.[7]

Figure 9.1 *Physical exercise cues the building blocks of learning in the brain*

The vital importance of sleep

Regular sleep has always been recognised as a vital component of good health both for children and adults. From experience it is evident that children's requirements for sleep change. They are affected by the seasons, hormones related to growth spurts (highly evident in teenagers, but often not acknowledged in early childhood), infections or illness, levels of physical activity and stress. By the time children reach two years old, the majority will have spent more time asleep than awake and generally most will spend forty per cent of their childhood asleep. Sleep is especially important for young children as it directly impacts both mental and physical development. Studies worldwide, which accumulated evidence from the fields of psychology, neurology and health, indicate that a lack of sleep in childhood leads to a number of impairments especially related to learning. We know as adults how tiredness affects our thinking, reasoning, behaviour, attention and self-control. Additionally, new evidence is now suggesting a possible link between the lack of sleep in childhood and obesity.

From my own experience and countless conversations with early years students it appears that there are increasing demands made on practitioners in early years settings to limit or prevent young children from sleeping. These requests to minimise or avert sleep are made by parents for children from babies upwards, and settings need to address this difficult situation professionally and with a clear policy that supports the child's rights and need to sleep as part of healthy development.

This issue was raised by baby room practitioners who took part in a research project. Their responses demonstrated the difficulties they faced in trying to balance the needs of the babies with that of their parents. The early years framework and Ofsted's regulation of settings make little mention of sleep, simply that a space for rest should be made available. Having spoken at length with parents the general consensus seems to suggest that any sleep in the day will disrupt sleep patterns at night. There is no evidence to suggest that daytime naps, regardless of their duration, have any effect on bedtime routines, unless they continue until late into the afternoon. In fact, I would argue that without the restorative morning or lunchtime nap young children become so overtired and hyper-stimulated that it can negatively affect any established sleep routines. Additionally the added stress within a room of numerous tired, crying young children or babies will undoubtedly trigger increased levels of cortisol levels within the brain. Unfortunately, when the body's stress response is activated repeatedly, the child has little chance of returning it to normal, resulting in damaging chronic stress. Interestingly, psychiatrist Dr John Ratey suggests that regular exercise and physical activity can release a number of neurochemicals in the brain that can help reverse the process of toxic stress, physically strengthening the brain's architecture.

It was not so long ago that babies were regularly wheeled into the garden in large prams to sleep in the fresh air, a practice still continued today in many Scandinavian nurseries and preschools. Acceptance of the health benefits of fresh air was universally accepted, extending into schools and hospitals that promoted sleeping or resting on camp beds, and not simply in the summer. A local hospital that specialised in the treatment of TB and other lung conditions provided open-air wards and direct access through gardens to the beach. Daily contact with the sea air throughout the year was considered the best treatment to aid recovery, and patients slept many a night under covered verandas. Again we must ask ourselves how our perceptions of health and lifestyle have changed, and consider the negative consequences of keeping children for long periods indoors in centrally heated, confined spaces. Again we are reminded of the legacy left by the crusading work of the McMillan sisters as they worked and campaigned to improve the health of the poorest children in Bradford and Deptford.

> Every child in the Nursery School is expected to sleep, or at least to rest, after dinner. Occasionally the mothers ask us if their children may be excused the sleep, but we make no exception to this rule, and they soon find that the mid-day nap does not interfere with the children's rest at nights. The two-year-old will sometimes sleep soundly for two hours – the three-year-old for an hour or an hour and a half. Some of the 'fours' or just turned 'fives' do not sleep, but lie quietly for at least three quarters of an hour. Only under very exceptional circumstances do we wake our children from the mid-day sleep.[8]

A healthy diet

A car needs fuel, water and oil to run smoothly. The fuel, of course, is the most important and frequent topping up of the tank is required. However, regular checks of the other essential components that allow the engine to function well – the oil and water – must be undertaken. In the same way food is not simply the fuel that provides power and energy; it needs to supply the important vitamins, minerals and oils that maintain and repair our complex bodies. It is impossible therefore to consider the term 'school readiness' without discussing diet and nutrition. The past twenty years has seen an alarming increase in the UK of childhood obesity, with data collected in 2012 indicating that one in five children are overweight or obese by the age of three.[9] Conversely, running alongside this, a growing number of children in the UK are now suffering from malnutrition caused by poor diets with limited fresh food or essential minerals. In order to produce the energy required to move, grow and learn, young children need regular small portions of nourishing food and plenty of water or milk. A new voluntary guide for early years settings, *Eat Better, Start Better*, has been developed to help providers and practitioners to meet the Early Years Foundation Stage welfare requirement by providing healthy, balanced and nutritious food and drink.

In the same way as regular maintenance of your car engine leads to fewer problems in the future, encouraging children in the Foundation years to establish healthy patterns and relationships with food will give them the energy and nutrients they need while they are growing rapidly. It also offers protection for their future long-term health. Practitioners will often suggest that the child's diet is up to the parent, but practitioners have a responsibility and a part to play in promoting, encouraging and developing habits for healthier lives. A mixed diet should provide all of the different proteins, carbohydrates, fats, vitamins and minerals a young child needs. Dietary patterns can run in families so working together with projects such as the allotment project described in Chapter 6 can make huge differences in a whole community. In terms of learning, making small changes in nutrition can rapidly increase concentration and energy levels, thereby increasing children's learning potential and physicality.

Research confirms that healthy eating habits in the years before school are very important because they influence growth, development and academic achievement in later life.[10]

'Inspire' and 'aspire' others

The London Olympics opened with the legacy that, after the games had been and gone, something would remain to motivate and inspire a new generation in Great Britain. The children, families and communities that watched the athletes were given a small glimpse into the training, diet and dedication required to reach the height of their sport. Alongside this they displayed the characteristics of team work, persistence, motivation, respect, friendship and participation. These surely are the characteristics for a happy and successful life? We all need to consider these aspirations and combine them into our work to support children, families and communities to become more actively involved. The following short case study demonstrates how knowledgeable early years practitioners with drive, enthusiasm and passion can drive forward changes and inspire others in the team.

As a pack away setting we were thrilled to receive a substantial sum of money to design a garden that was to be solely used by our preschool children. We worked tiredlessly to create the perfect garden, went on courses, made a scrap book and had a grand opening. After so much hard work, it was difficult to reflect on our work and realise that we had got it so wrong. As lovely as the garden was, it was representative of what the adults wanted. There was no doubt in anyone's minds that it had been designed with the children's needs in mind; however, we had failed to provide an outdoor environment that could fulfil and stretch the physical needs of the children. The outcome of such a mistake was conflict between the adults as how best to use the garden and worst of all the garden soon lost its appeal for the children, with accessing the garden being a requirement rather than an experience. As a leader I struggled to motivate my team as I was not confident in my abilities to put things right and to be honest had no inspiration or motivation to make the changes, not to mention being too tired as I ploughed my way through my Early Years Foundation Degree.

As it turns out the Foundation Degree was my inspiration and as I moved into the second year my motivation to revamp the garden became stronger and the daunting task became more achievable. Through amazing tutors and extremely supportive study colleagues, I developed the confidence, knowledge, techniques and practice that enabled me, along with the other owners of the preschool, to motivate the team, direct them through the vision and articulate how we, adults and children, were going to undertake this enormous transformation. Like all good practitioners we started with observations, which soon told us exactly what the problem was. The children just wanted to dig and our digging area was very small and situated in a corner of the garden that could get extremely hot in the sunshine. It was just too small and did not inspire the children at all. Another area, the sensory garden, was underused. It was far too big and in an area which, even when the sun did shine, was always in the shade. Nothing grew and the children only went in there to retrieve their footballs. So we decided to change them around. We divided the children into garden working groups and every session, come rain and shine, a different group of children with several adults would go down to the garden to do some 'garden work' as we called it. We kept the parents up to date with pictures of the progress and it soon become the talking point of the preschool. I was so proud of the transformation that was taking place. The children, parents and staff were totally motivated to complete the work and I clearly remember sitting with my partner, excitedly relaying all the changes and our vision for a mud kitchen and feeling such a burning passion and emotion as we talked through some of the ideas that we had planned for the newly revamped digging area.

The digging area is now a big space where all types of magical and inspirational play can be observed daily. Old kitchen units are great for a 'mud pie' kitchen (although eventually we would like a disused real oven and belfast sink), but the old tyres, bread crates and various other odds and ends provide endless play opportunities. The children understand that wellies and waterproofs must be worn, particularly in the muddier areas. The sensory area is well on its way and now provides a more exploratory experience. We have managed to grow tomatoes, beans and strawberries and it is wonderful to see the equipment and resources that we bought when we first established the garden finally being used by the children. The result is now a garden that is full of awe and wonder, curiosity, fascination and lots of fun. We will continue to develop the garden to fully meet our vision, but with renewed inspiration, motivation and passion we feel anything is possible.

Again, the words of Peters at the start of the chapter ring true in this example from practice. 'Worthwhile things cannot be forced on reluctant minds. They are acquired by contact with those who have already acquired them and who have patience, zeal and competence enough to initiate others into them.'

Finally, I end the chapter and the book with the inspiring words from Lord Coe's opening speech at the London Olympic Games:

> [H]istory has prepared us for today. For us too, for every Briton ... this is our time, and one day we will tell our children and our grandchildren that when our time came, we did it right.[11]

I urge you to think carefully about your work with children. You can change lives and shape futures. History has prepared us and given us the ammunition for the fight and now we must act and, most importantly, make sure that we 'do it right'.

Challenges and dilemmas

- Resist the top-down pressure to prepare children with structured 'school'-based activities.
- Ensure children are physically active for a minimum of three hours each day.

- Think carefully about how you are developing the dispositions of learning such as perseverance, determination and self-reliance.
- Support children to take risks, be adventurous and work as a team.
- Consider writing a sleep policy that supports young children's need for rest, and to protect children's rights to sleep.
- Think carefully about the snacks or meals provided by the setting.
- Use the guidance *Eat Better, Start Better* to inform portion sizes and menus.
- Reflect on the possibilities and inspirations within your community. How could you use these to arouse children's interests?
- What can be changed in your outside area to add intrigue, challenge, and awe and wonder?

Epilogue

There is growing acceptance that the first seven years of life are critical, with increasing evidence supporting fundamental links between physical development and young children's health, well-being and later achievements. However, in order to further develop and embed this prime area, practitioners need to recognise the crucial role they play in the development of the whole child.

The main aim of this book has been to help practitioners rethink their work with young children, focusing more clearly on the importance of health and physical development. This new emphasis on developing healthy habits for life in the Foundation years cannot be understated; we must all now recognise the links between health and future development. The book shares examples of good practice in order to make us re-examine our practice. It also introduces the notion that children have health rights: to play outdoors, not in safety surfaced deserts, but in wild exciting places or community spaces that open up possibilities; to sleep regularly and when required, rather than have time set by the needs of an adult; and to have access to small, regular meals that contain the vital nutrients necessary for growth, energy and vitality. We are quite literally shaping the future for these children and so what we offer now will determine not only their future health but fundamentally their happiness and life chances.

The first chapter started with key words from the Marmot review, *Fair Society, Healthy Lives*. It is the job of each and every one of us working with young children and families to make it our highest priority to '*give every child the best start in life*'. I hope that this book enables you to see the potential in every child, to be brave in your approach and to light the fire of achievement in yourself and all the children you encounter.

Notes

Introduction to the series

1 National Association for the Education of Young Children. Position statement, 2009.
2 DfES, *The Early Years Foundation Stage*. London: DfES, 2007.

Introduction to *The Growing Child*

1 C. Tickell, *The Early Years: Foundations for Life, Health and Learning – An Independent Report on the Early Years Foundation Stage to Her Majesty's Government*. 2011.
2 C. Ball, *Start Right: The Importance of Early Learning* (The Start Right Report). London: Royal Society for the Encouragement of Arts, Manufactures and Commerce, 1994.
3 *The Foundations of Lifelong Health are Built in Early Childhood*. Centre on The Developing Child, Harvard University, 2010.

1 Setting the scene

1 Sir Michael Marmot, *Fair Society, Healthy Lives: Strategic Review of Health Inequalities*. The Marmot Review, 2010.
2 L. Pound, in J. Fisher, *Foundations of Learning*. Open University Press, 2003, ch. 1.
3 Supported by evidence from organisations such as Play England, PLAYLINK, the Health and Safety Executive and Government departments.
4 K. Duberry, 'Risk Taking and Achievements Outdoors', *Early Childhood Practice* 3.1 (2001), pp. 67–70. S. Tishman, E. Jay and D. N. Perkins, 'Teaching Thinking Dispositions: From Transmission to Enculturation', *Theory into Practice* 32 (Summer 1993), pp. 147–53.
5 R. Shore, 'What Have We Learned?' in *Rethinking the Brain*. New York: Families and Work Institute, 1997.
6 S. Greenfield, *The Human Brain: A Guided Tour*. Phoenix, 1997.
7 C. Tickell, *The Early Years: Foundations for Life, Health and Learning. An Independent Report on the Early Years Foundation Stage to Her Majesty's Government*. DfE, 2011.
8 *The Foundation Years: Preventing Poor Children Becoming Poor Adults*. UK Govt., 2010.
9 Marmot Review, *Fair Society, Healthy Lives: Strategic Review of Health Inequalities*. UK Dept of Health, 2010.
10 K. Sylva, E. Melhuish, P. Sammons, I. Siraj-Blatchford and B. Taggart (eds.), *Early Childhood Matters: Evidence from the Effective Pre-school and Primary Education Project*. Oxford: Routledge, 2010.
11 G. Claxton and M. Carr, 'A Framework for Teaching Learning: The Dynamics of Disposition', *Early Years* 24.1 (2004), pp. 87–97.
12 C. Ball, *Start Right: The Importance of Early Learning*. Royal Society for the Encouragement of Arts, Manufacture and Commerce, 1994.

2 Play and exploration

1 British Heart Foundation National Centre for Physical Activity and Health, Loughborough University, 2011.
2 UK Department for Children, Schools and Families, 2008; Department for Education, 2012.
3 C. Tickell, *The Early Years: Foundations for Life, Health and Learning. An Independent Report on the Early Years Foundation Stage to Her Majesty's Government*. DfE, 2011.
4 UN Convention on the Rights of the Child 1989.
5 M. McMillan, *The Child and the State*. Manchester: National Labour Press, 1911.
6 T. Bruce, *Early Childhood Education*. 3rd edition. London: Hodder and Stoughton, 2005.
7 Claxton and Carr, 'A Framework for Teaching Learning'.
8 Anthony Pellegrini and Peter K. Smith, 'Physical Activity Play: The Nature and Function of a Neglected Aspect of Playing', *Child Development* 69 (1998), pp. 577–98.
9 *Good Practice in the Early Years Foundation Stage*. DCfS, 2009.
10 D. Selleck, 'Baby Art, Art is Me', Refocus Collection, 1997, www.sightlines-initative.com
11 S. Nicholson, 'How Not to Cheat Children: The Theory of Loose Parts', *Landscape Architecture* (October 1971).
12 T. Gill, *No Fear: Growing up in a Risk Adverse Society*. London: Calouste Gulbenkian Foundation, 2007.
13 Dr Len Almond, *UK Physical Activity Guidelines for Early Years*. BHF National Centre Physical Activity & Health, Loughborough University, 2011.
14 C. Steedman, *Childhood Culture and Class in Britain*. London: Virago Press, 1990, p. 193.
15 Daniel Goleman, *Emotional Intelligence: Why it Can Matter More than IQ*. London: Bloomsbury Publishing, 1996.
16 Adapted from Tina Bruce, *Early Childhood Education*. London: Hodder & Stoughton, 1987.
17 C. Steedman, *Childhood Culture and Class in Britain*. London: Virago Press, 1990.
18 M. Montessori, *The Absorbent Mind*. Adyar, India: The Theosophical Publishing House, 1946.
19 E. Lawrence, 'The Malting House School', *National Froebel Foundation Bulletin* 5 (1949), pp. 1–6.
20 M. J. Drummond, 'Comparisons in Early Years Education: History, Fact, and Fiction', *Early Childhood Research and Practice* 2.1 (2000).
21 A. Sigman, 'The Impact of Screen Media on Children: A Eurovision for Parliament'. Presentation given to The Quality of Childhood Group, 2011.
22 T. Gill, *No Fear: Growing Up in a Risk Averse Society*. Calouste Gulbenkian Foundation, 2007.
23 A. Sigman, *The Spoilt Generation: Standing up to our Demanding Children*. London: Little Brown and Co., 2009.
24 R. Garrick, C. Bath, K. Dunn, H. Maconochie, B. Willis and C. Wolstenholme, *Children's Experiences of the Early Years Foundation Stage*. DfE, 2011.

3 Active learning

1 J. Santer, C. Griffiths and D. Goodall, *Free Play in Early Childhood: A Literature Review*. National Children's Bureau, 2007.
2 C. Stephen, *Playing, Doing, Thinking and Learning*. Stirling Institute of Education, 2007.
3 Claxton and Carr, 'A Framework for Teaching Learning'.
4 D. Corbetta and E. Thelen, 'Lateral Biases and Fluctuations in Infants' Spontaneous Arm Movements and Reaching', *Developmental Psychobiology* 34 (1999), pp. 237–55.
5 Highscope ReSource, Spring 2011.
6 GB, DCSF, EYFS, '4:2 Learning and Developing', 2008. This emphasis has now been strengthened further in the new EYFS (2012) with Active Learning identified as one of the three characteristics of effective learning and teaching.
7 Curriculum for Excellence. Scotland: HMIe, 2010.
8 The Foundation Phase, Framework for Children's Learning for 3 to 7-year-olds in Wales. Department for Children, Education, Lifelong Learning and Skills: Welsh Assembly Government, 2008.
9 M. Schickedanz et al., in J. Doherty and M. Hughes, *Child Development Theory and Practice 0–11*. London: Pearson Longman, 1993.

10 L. S. Vygotsky, *Mind in Society: The Development of Higher Psychological Processes*. Cambridge: Harvard University Press, 1978.

11 R. Tharpe and R. Gallimore, *Rousing Minds to Life: Teaching, Learning, and Schooling in Social Context*. Cambridge: Cambridge University Press, 1988.

12 J. Bruner, *The Process of Education*, revised edition. New York: Harvard University Press, 1977.

13 GB, DCSF, *The Early Years Foundation Stage Framework*. DCfS, 2007.

14 Adapted from Chambers and Sugden 2006, in Maria Evangelou, Kathy Sylva and Maria Kyriacou, *Early Years Learning and Development Literature Review*. Department of Education, University of Oxford, 2009.

4 Creating and thinking critically

1 Margaret McMillan, *The Nursery School*. London: J. M. Dent and Sons, 1930.

2 S. A. Goddard Blythe, *Attention, Balance and Coordination: The A,B,C of Learning Success*. Chichester: Wiley-Blackwell, 2009.

3 S. Goddard Blythe, *What Babies and Children REALLY Need*. Stroud: Hawthorn Press, 2008.

4 Goddard Blythe, *What Babies and Children REALLY Need*.

5 M. Montessori, *The Absorbent Mind*. Adyar, India: The Theosophical Publishing House.

6 http://www.jabadao.org/?p=developmental.movement.play.research

7 S. Brice Heath, *Play in Nature: The Foundation of Creative Thinking*, ch. 11. Born Creative, DEMOS, 2010.

8 50things@nationaltrust.org.uk

9 http://www.sightlines-initiative.com/images/Library/our_first_explorations/death_fear_bravado.pdf

10 Tim Loughton and Sarah Teather, *Creating the Conditions: Trusted Professional and Targeted Resources for Creativity in the Early Years*, ch. 3. Born Creative, DEMOS, 2010.

5 Building developing confidence

1 Montessori, *The Absorbent Mind*.

2 J. Ayres, *Sensory Integration and the Child: Understanding Hidden Sensory Challenges*. Western Psychological Services, 2005.

3 J. P. Shonkoff, W. T. Boyce and B. S. McEwen, 'Neuroscience, Molecular Biology, and the Childhood Roots of Health Disparities: Building a New Framework for Health Promotion and Disease Prevention', *JAMA* 301 (2009), pp. 2252–59.

4 *The Foundations of Lifelong Health are Built in Early Childhood*. Centre for the Developing Child, Harvard University, 2010.

5 M. Evangelou et al., *Early Years Learning and Development Literature Review*. DfE, 2009. The Physical Development section of the review draws heavily on the work of Maude, Chambers and Sugden.

6 G. Rapley and T. Murkett, *Baby Led Weaning: Helping your Baby to Love Good Food*. Vermillion, 2008.

7 World Health Organisation (WHO), *Global Strategy for Infant and Young Child Feeding*. http://www.who.int/nutrition/topics/global_strategy/en/index.html

8 HM Government, *Maternity and Early Years: Making a Good Start to Family Life*. London: DfE/DH, 2010.

9 C. Tickell, *The Early Years: Foundations for Life, Health and Learning*. An Independent Report on the Early Years Foundation Stage to Her Majesty's Government, 2011.

10 Montessori, *The Absorbent Mind*.

11 M. E. Chambers and D. A. Sugden, *Early Years Movement Skills: Description, Diagnosis and Intervention*. London: Whurr, 2006.

12 Chambers and Sugden, *Early Years Movement Skills*.

13 EYFS card, Active Learning 4.2. GB, DCSF, EYFS, 4:2 Learning and Developing, 2008.

14 Practice Guidance for EYFS 2008: 79.

15 Mordy and Hess 1964, as cited in K. Mathieson, 'Hand in Hand: Physical and Behavioural Development,' *Early Education* 67 (Summer 2012).

6 Engaging families

1 *Supporting Families in the Foundation Years.* DfE, DH, 2011.
2 C. Ball, *Start Right: The Importance of Early Learning.* London: Royal Society for the Encouragement of Arts, Manufactures and Commerce, 1994.
3 Sir Michael Marmot, *Fair Society, Healthy Lives: Strategic Review of Health Inequalities.* The Marmot Review, 2010.
4 *Gardening in Schools: A Vital Tool for Children's Learning.* Royal Horticultural Society, 2007.
5 T. Newman, *What Works in Building Resilience.* Barnardos Policy and Research Unit, 2004.
6 F. Leuven, *Well-being and Involvement in Care Settings: A Process-oriented Self-evaluation Instrument.* Kind & Gezin and Research Centre for Experiential Education, 2005.
7 The Good Childhood Report, *A Review of our Children's Well-being.* The Children's Society, 2012.

7 The different worlds of boys and girls

1 P. Holland, *We Don't Play With Guns Here: War, Weapons and Superhero Play in the Early Years.* Maidenhead: Open University Press, 2003.
2 T. Gill, *No Fear: Growing up in a Risk Averse Society.* London: Calouste Gulbenkian Foundation, 2007.
3 C. Fine, *Delusions of Gender: The Real Science Behind Sex Differences.* London: Icon Books, 2011.
4 S. Biddulph, *Raising Boys.* London: Harper Thorsons, 2003.
5 Boys Development Project, Manchester City Council Sure Start Projects, 2011.
6 H. Ward, 'Today Children, We are Taking Risks', *The Times Educational Supplement,* 6 June 2008.
7 http://www.playpods.co.uk
8 J. Bronowski, *The Ascent of Man.* BBC Books, 2011.
9 B. Lucas and G. Claxton, *New Kinds of Smart: How the Science of Learnable Intelligence is Changing Education.* Maidenhead: Open University Press, 2010.
10 M. Gurian, *Boys and Girls Learn Differently.* San Francisco: Jossey-Bass, 2001.
11 Julia Donaldson, *Tyrannosaurus Drip.* London: Macmillan, 2007.
12 Tickell, *The Early Years: Foundations for Life, Health and Learning.*
13 C. Nutbrown, *Foundations for Quality: The Independent Review of Early Education and Childcare Qualifications. Final Report.* DfE, 2012.
14 S. Biddulph, Raising Boys. London: Harper Thorsons, 2003.
15 P. Holland, *We Don't Play With Guns Here: War, Weapons and Superhero Play in the Early Years.* Maidenhead: Open University Press.
16 *Confident, Capable and Creative: Supporting Boys' Achievements.* Guidance for practitioners in the Early Years Foundation Stage. DCFS, 2007.

8 Forest School

1 D. Sobel, *Wild Play.* San Francisco: Sierra Club Books, 2011.
2 T. Gill, 'Now for Free-range Childhood'. *The Guardian,* 2 April 2009. www.guardian.co.uk/commentisfree/2009/apr/02/children-safety
3 www.thelancet.com. Published online 18 July 2012. http://dx.doi.org/10.1016/S0140-6736(12)60954-4
4 Centers for Disease Control and Prevention. Surgeon General's Report on Physical Activity and Health. 1996. http://www.cdc.gov/nccdphp/sgr/ index.htm (accessed 4 June 2012).
5 Report to Natural England on Childhood and Nature, *A Survey on Changing Relationships with Nature across Generations.* Childhood and Nature, 2009.
6 R. Louv, *Last Child in the Woods: Saving Our Children from Nature-Deficit Disorder.* Chapel Hill: Algonquin Books, 2005.
7 E. O. Wilson, *Biophilia: The Human Bond with Other Species.* Cambridge: Harvard University Press, 1984.
8 S. Moss, *Natural Childhood.* National Trust, 2012.
9 *The Good Childhood Report.* The Children's Society, 2012.

10 J. Piaget, *The Principles of Genetic Epistemology*. London: Routledge and Kegan Paul.

11 L. O'Brien and R. Murray, *Such Enthusiasm: A Joy to See. An Evaluation of Forest School in England*. 2005. Available at: http://www.forestresearch.gov.uk (accessed 18 August 2012).

12 Forest Education Initiative, 2005. An initiative led by The Forest School Association, the new Forest School professional organisation for the UK.

13 K. Milchem, 'Breaking Through the Concrete: The Emergence of Forest School in London', in S. Knight (ed.), *Forest School For All*. London: Sage, 2011.

14 B. Hughes, *A Playworker's Taxonomy of Play Types*. London: Playlink UK, 1996.

15 T. Byron, as cited in *The Outdoor Environment: How Can our Children Learn to Care about their Futures?* The Learning Escape, 2012.

16 Ed Balls, 'Every Child Matters', speech to the National Children's Bureau at the launch of 'Staying Safe', 23 July 2007.

17 Penny Wilson, Play Association Tower Hamlets, quoted in *The Guardian*, 28 September 2010, http://www.guardian.co.uk/society/2010/sep/28/back-to-nature-inner-city-children

18 P. Graham, *Susan Isaacs: A Life Freeing the Minds of Children*. London: Karnac Books, 2009.

9 Ready for school or prepared for life?

1 R. S. Peters, 'Aims of Education—A Conceptual Inquiry', in (ed.), *Philosophy of Education*. Oxford: Oxford University Press, 1973.

2 R. Alexander, *Children, their World, their Education*. London: Routledge, 2010.

3 P. Dixon, *Let Me Be*. PECHE LUNA, 2005.

4 C. Ball, *The Importance of Early Learning*. The Royal Society for the Encouragement of Arts, Manufacture and Commerce (RSA), 1994.

5 D. Elkind, 'The Power of Play: Learning What Comes Naturally', *American Journal of Play* 1.1 (Summer 2008), pp. 1–6.

6 J. Ratey, *Spark: The Revolutionary New Science of Exercise and the Brain*. New York: Little Brown and Co, 2008.

7 L. Karsten, 'It All Used to be Better? Different Generations on Continuity and Change in Urban Children's Daily Use of Time and Space', *Children's Geographies: Advancing Interdisciplinary Understanding of Young People's Lives* 3.3 (2005), pp. 271–74.

8 E. Stevinson, *The Open Air Nursery School*. London: J. M. Dent and Sons, 1923.

9 Report of the Children and Young People's Health Outcomes Forum, 2012.

10 *Eat Better, Start Better: Voluntary Food and Drink Guidelines for Early Years Settings in England – A Practical Guide*. School Food Trust, 2012.

11 S. Coe, Opening Speech London Olympic Games, 2012.

Author index

Subject index